CONTENTS

[Figures within brackets refer to entry numbers]

FOREWORD

The decade 1960—1970 occasioned a marked expansion in the field of linguistics. Academically, curricula in the subject were added in many universities both on the graduate and undergraduate levels. The number of published works in pure linguistics increased as well as the number of studies linking linguistic points of view with other fields, e.g., psycholinguistics. A number of new journals appeared.

This increased activity has naturally attracted people, both students and teachers, who are approaching linguistics for the first time. Because of the diverse views, heated debates and rapid development that characterizes any active science, it is especially well that there be some orientation to the basic works. Miss Wawrzyszko has aptly filled this need with her annotated bibliography. I predict it will find wide and appreciative use.

Philip W. Davis
Linguistics Committee
Rice University
Houston, Texas

June 1970

PREFACE

This work was begun with the thought of assisting the faculty and students of linguistics of the Departments of Modern Languages and of English at Simon Fraser University.

I wish to thank, first of all, Dr. Philip W. Davis of the Linguistics Committee, Rice University, Houston, Texas, formerly of Simon Fraser University. I am greatly indebted to him for introducing me to the subject of American linguistics and to the major linguistic publications, and for the critical reading of my manuscript.

I sincerely appreciate the interest and advice given me by many members of the Department of Modern Languages at Simon Fraser University. My very special thanks go to Dr. G. L. Bursill-Hall for helping me find my way among the grammarians and their complicated theories, as much as for his assistance in arranging some portions of my work.

I wish to express my heartfelt thanks to my former professor of linguistics, Dr. M. Szymczak of Warsaw University, now with the University of Alberta on an international exchange teaching post. Dr. Szymczak kindly devoted much of his time to discussing with me an overall view of linguistics today. He has also helped me with the first organization of my bibliographical material into the appropriate chapters.

I owe a debt of gratitude to Mrs. Philipa Polson of the English Department, Simon Fraser University, for her advice on the literary aspects of linguistics, especially on stylistics.

I am deeply grateful to the staff in all divisions of the Simon Fraser University Library, particularly to Miss Margaret Briggs, for counsel, cooperation and countless kindnesses.

I would especially like to acknowledge the help and encouragement received from my colleagues, Eugene Bridwell and Daniel

Bruce. They both share credit for bringing this book to existence. My indebtness to them cannot be adequately expressed.

Among the many persons who assisted in this undertaking, but who cannot all be mentioned here, are the graduate students in linguistics at Simon Fraser University. I would like to thank them for their contributions to my better understanding of the field and of their needs as future users of the bibliography.

For whatever are the shortcomings, I alone am responsible. I could not follow all the suggestions. Faced with the labyrinth of a subject, I made the final decision on the content and form of this presentation, hoping to serve many readers as soon as possible.

Aleksandra K. Wawrzyszko

Simon Fraser University
Burnaby, British Columbia
June 1970

INTRODUCTION

This bibliography aims at all linguists and students of linguistics, particularly those beyond the introductory university level. It embraces basic publications in the field to date, focusing on works of the mid- and late 1960's. Special attention is devoted to a fairly comprehensive presentation of standard information sources in linguistic research: bibliographies, dictionaries, glossaries, directories, abstracting and indexing services.

The bibliography contains more than three hundred annotated entries of monographs and series as well as periodicals concerned primarily with British and American linguistics. Exception has been made to include a number of influential works by non-English scholars (e.g. de Saussure, Martinet, Jespersen, Trubetzkoy) whose contributions to general linguistics, in its Anglo-American aspect, were either written in English, translated into English, or appeared in learned multi-lingual serial publications, such as *Travaux Linguistiques de Prague.*

The volume presents fundamentals of all topics comprising the science of linguistics and discusses not only historical development, scientific methods of language description and linguistic analysis, together with semantic, grammatical, and phonetic systems, but also various theories of language created by different schools of thought (Geneva, Prague, London, MIT). It also includes some representation of applied linguistics in its computational and machine translation aspects.

Because this work illustrates the interrelationships between language and other disciplines—literature, philosophy, psychology, anthropology, and sociology—all of which are relevant to linguistics and essential to widening of human communications, it is hoped that it will be useful, in some measure, to students and teachers of English literary history, to those concerned with

xi

physical and psychological properties of speech and public speaking, to philosophers, sociologists, anthropologists, and to all interested laymen in general.

As the bibliography was not intended to be comprehensive, certain areas of interest such as dialectology or language laboratory materials have been generally omitted.

Cross-references are provided in order to best utilize the content within the frame of this work.

Author and periodical indexes are also supplied. The first includes editors and a few selected dictionaries, known only by their titles; the second includes series, serial bibliographies, abstracts, indexes and theses. Numbers refer to entries.

Bibliographies and bibliographical footnotes included in the books under review are noted together with other characteristic features such as glossaries or maps, following the descriptive parts of the monographs. Journals are discussed with references to their primary indexing and abstracting sources.

I
GENERAL SOURCES
AND SELECTED SPECIAL TOPICS

ABBREVIATIONS

Schwartz, Robert J. *The Complete Dictionary of Abbreviations.*
New York, Crowell [1959, c1955] 211 p.   1

> Contains over 25,000 entries in the fields of business, law,
> religion, engineering, book trade, Army, Navy, U. S. govern-
> ment agencies, stock market, shipping, medicine, and other
> subjects. Includes societies, institutions and degrees. *Use:*
> Intended for writers, speakers, businessmen, scientists,
> teachers, students, librarians, secretaries, and general users.

Thomas, Robert C., James M. Ethridge and Frederick G. Ruffner,
Jr., eds. *Acronyms and Initialisms Dictionary; a guide to*   2
alphabetic designations, contractions, acronyms, initialisms,
and similar condensed appelations; covering: aerospace, associations, biochemistry, business and trade, domestic and international affairs, education, electronics, genetics, government,
labor, medicine, military, pharmacy, physiology, politics, religion, science, societies, sports, technical drawings and specifica-
tions, transportation, and other fields. 2d ed. Contributing
editors: Edwin B. Steen [and others] Detroit, Gale Research
Co. [1965] 767 p.

Ulving, Tor, comp. *Periodica Philologica Abbreviata.* A list of
initial abbreviations of periodicals in philology and related   3
subjects. Stockholm, Almqvist & Wiksell, 1963. 137 p.

> A very useful list of abbreviations for international publica-
> tions, containing over 3,200 entries. Gives names of periodi-
> cals and places of publication. Abbreviations in Cyrillic and

Greek are transcribed according to the Swedish library system. Includes abbreviations of institutions and societies, the names of which often appear abbreviated, and also abbreviations of some nonperiodical works, such as dictionaries and text editions, which are often referred to by abbreviations.

DIRECTORIES

Contemporary Authors; the international bio-bibliographical guide to current authors and their works. v.1- 1962- Detroit, Gale Research.

4

International in scope, semi-annual publication listing bio-bibliographies of current writers in the fields of humanities, sciences, and social sciences. Includes a fair number of linguists. Gives: personal data, career (education, positions, society memberships, honors), writings (attempts at a comprehensive bibliography), work in progress, sidelights, and sometimes biographical sources. Cumulative indexes every two years.

Directory of American Scholars; a biographical directory. 5th ed. Edited by the Jacques Cattell Press. New York, R. R. Bowker, 1969. 4 vols. Published with the cooperation of the American Council of Learned Societies.

5

Contents. -v.3. *Foreign languages (modern and classical), linguistics and philology.*

A biographical encyclopedia of scholars in the United States and Canada, including linguists, literary men, research workers, recognized editors, speakers, and teachers at college and university levels. Gives personal data, education, overall field of specialization, positions, society memberships, items of research or interest; often publications with the name of publisher and publication date, articles with the name of journal and date; and address. General index in the 4th volume. *See also* 157.

4

BIBLIOGRAPHIES, ABSTRACTS, INDEXES

Allen, Harold B., comp. *Linguistics and English Linguistics.* New York, Appleton-Century-Crofts [1966] 108 p. (Goldentree bibliographies) **6**

A selective bibliography of books and articles listed under the headings: Bibliographies, Dictionaries and Glossaries, Festschriften and Miscellaneous Collections, Linguistics, English Language and English Linguistics, Language Instruction, and Special Topics; with further sub-divisions. Includes author index. *Use:* For graduate and advanced undergraduate students in English, education, linguistics, and related subjects.

Allen, Virginia F. and Sidney Forman. *English as a Second Language; a comprehensive bibliography.* New York, Teachers College Press [1967] 255 p. **7**

A computer-produced book catalog of monographs, periodicals, films, filmstrips, phonograph records, tapes, and related materials located in the Teachers College Library, Columbia University. Classified by subject: 'Linguistics' (incl. general; syntax and morphology; phonology); 'Language culture area' (incl. cultural descriptions and communications; semantics); 'Language learning' (incl. research methods, testing, educational technology); 'Texts' (incl. general, and specific languages); 'Reference' (incl. dictionaries, bibliographies, publishers' catalogs). Provided for each item are: author, title, edition, place, publisher, date, paging, illustrations, series notes, price, and language of book. Author title and publisher indexes. *Use:* Although concerned primarily with the study and teaching of English as a foreign or second language, it contains much information on most aspects of general linguistics, English and American.

Alston, Robin C., comp. *A Bibliography of the English Language from the Invention of Printing to the Year 1800;* A Systematic Record of Writings on English, Based on the Collections of the Principal Libraries of the World. Leeds, Printed for the author by E. J. Arnold, 1965- (In progress) **8**

A multivolume work in progress. Lists and gives locations for books in major libraries of the world, focuses on those in the

U. K. and the U. S. A. Projected to include 20 volumes, this set will cover all aspects of languages. Contents: v.1. English grammars written in English and English grammar written in Latin by native speakers. v. 2. Polyglot dictionaries and grammars [...] v. 4. Spelling books. v. 5. The English dictionary. v. 7. Logic, philosophy, epistemology, universal language. v. 8. Treatises on short-hand. Includes bibliographies.

9 Bailey, Richard W. and Dolores M. Burton. *English Stylistics: A Bibliography.* Cambridge, Mass., MIT Press [1968] 198 p.

Contains some 1,700 partially annotated entries covering: bibliographic sources; language and style before 1900; English stylistics in the twentieth century, and an introductory chapter on English stylistics in the mid-twentieth century. Deals with various theories of style and methods of style analysis together with references to individual writers of literary works. Indexes.

10 Bursill-Hall, G. L. *Bibliography: Theories of Syntactic Analysis.* In *Studies in Linguistics*, v. 16, 1962. pp. 100-112.

11 Centre for Information on Language Teaching. *A Language-Teaching Bibliography;* compiled and edited by the Centre for Information on Language Teaching and the English-Teaching Information Centre of the British Council. Cambridge, University Press, 1968. 243 p.

International in coverage, this is a very useful annotated bibliography containing over 700 entries. Includes titles in linguistics, psychology and sociology, as well as grammars, dictionaries, and linguistic and methodological studies of specific languages. Consists of three parts dealing with: language (in general); language teaching; and particular languages (English, including English as a foreign language, French, German, Italian, Russian and Spanish). All annotations are in English. Author index. *Use:* For language teachers, text-book writers, educational administrators, research workers and librarians.

Dale, Edgar. *Bibliography of Vocabulary Studies.* [A revision] Columbus, Bureau of Educational Research and Service, Ohio State University, 1949. 101 p.   **12**

A very useful bibliography of books, periodical articles, theses, doctoral dissertations and abstracts in humanities, sciences, social sciences, and miscellaneous fields. Contains 1855 entries. Lists titles in twenty-five different categories. Includes sections on vocabulary contents of periodicals and pamphlets, newspapers, radio, motion pictures, and comics. (The second, revised edition of the above work, published in 1963, has not been examined by the compiler.)

Dingwall, William O. *Transformational Generative Grammar: A Bibliography.* [Washington, D. C.] Center for Applied Linguistics, 1965. 82 p.   **13**

A comprehensive, unannotated bibliography of books, periodical articles, dissertations and unpublished papers covering all aspects of the theory of transformational generative grammar. Contains 962 entries, arranged alphabetically and supplied with symbols indicating topical categories. Includes an index of languages and language families.

Ferguson, Charles A. and William A. Stewart, eds. *Linguistic Reading Lists for Teachers of Modern Languages: French, German, Italian, Russian, Spanish.* Authors: Frederick B. Agard [and others] Washington, D. C., Center for Applied Linguistics, 1963. 114 p.   **14**

A selective annotated bibliography containing book and periodical article references recommended for linguists, language teachers and librarians. Provides no items on language teaching methodology or related background material. Includes two brief, but valuable sections on general linguistics and English linguistics.

Hammer, John H. and Frank A. Rice, eds. *A Bibliography of Contrastive Linguistics.* [Washington] Center for Applied Linguistics, 1965. 41 p.   **15**

Based on the *Contrastive studies in linguistics: A bibliographical checklist,* by W. Gage, published in 1961. Covers works on comparative linguistics, featuring two or more languages.

Following a general section, the materials are listed alphabetically by foreign language. Author index.

16 Hays, David G. *Annotated Bibliography of Rand Publications in Computational Linguistics.* Santa Monica, Calif., Rand Corp., 1965. 25 p. (Rand Corporation, Memorandum RM-3894-1-PR)

Lists 93 Rand publications on linguistic theory, linguistic research methods, computational methods for linguistics, the Russian and English languages, information retrieval, automatic content analysis, psycholinguistics, and character readers. Does not include information theory in the sense of probabilistic analysis of communication channels, artificial intelligence, or nerve-net simulation. Indicates prices, sources of availability (besides RAND) and types of copies that can be supplied upon request. Includes lists of deposit libraries in the U. S. and those abroad, also a publication number index.

17 Kennedy, Arthur G. *A Bibliography of Writings on the English Language from the Beginning of Printing to the End of 1922.* New York, Hafner, 1961 [c1927] 517 p.

An important comprehensive bibliography of books, pamphlets and periodical articles, containing 13,402 entries. Includes numerous references to critical reviews. Divided into ten chapters: general collections; general and historical writings; English paleography; English and other languages; Anglo-Saxon or Old English; Middle English; modern English; recent tendencies in English; history of the study of the English language; theory and method of the study and teaching of English; with further subdivisions. Contains index of authors and reviewers, and index of subjects. *Use:* Excellent source of information to lecturers, researchers, students of English language and literary history.

18 Milic, Louis T. *Style and Stylistics; an analytical bibliography.* New York, The Free Press [1967] 199 p.

Contains over 800 entries, mainly in English and about English literature and language. Included also are works on linguistic philosophy, logic, psychology of perception and learning, mathematical linguistics, computer technology, sociology and anthropology. Arranged into five categories and listed chronologically within each part: Part 1, Theoretical; Part 2, Methodological; Part 3, Applied; Part 4, Bibliographies; Part 5, Omnibus. Supplied with cross-references and several indexes. *Use:* Originally intended for graduate courses in stylistics, it is a very useful source of information to teachers and students in English language (composition, grammar, etc.) and linguistics at all levels, also for those in psychology, logic, social sciences, translation, computer and information sciences.

Northup, Clark S. *A Register of Bibliographies of the English Language and Literature.* With contributions by Joseph Quincey Adams and Andrew Keogh. New York, Hafner, 1962 [1925] 507 p. **19**

Lists separate works and those appended to books and periodicals. Includes bibliographies on language and related subjects under the headings: language, English language, dictionaries, grammars, phonetics, etc.; with cross-references. Index. Still useful, especially for older and historical materials.

Nostrand, Howard Lee, David William Foster and Clay Benjamin Christensen. *Research on Language Teaching; an annotated international bibliography, 1945-64.* 2d ed., rev. Seattle, University of Washington Press, 1965. 373 p. (University of Washington publications on language and language learning, v. 1) **20**

Although intended primarily as a source of reference on research materials related to foreign language teaching, this volume contains much useful information on teaching and learning of English language and presents various aspects of linguistics in general. Divided into three parts: Pt. 1. Bibliographies. Pt. 2. Periodicals and serials. Pt. 3. Research completed and in progress. Part 3 is most extensive and deals with: methodology of research; methods, materials and equipment; auditory and visual aids; pyschology of language and language learning; linguistics; teaching the cultural and intercultural context; langues in the curriculum; teacher qualifications and training. Includes a directory of agencies, institutions, and organizations. Indexes.

21 Ohanessian, Sirarpi, ed. *Reference List of Materials for English as a Second Language.* Edited by Sirarpi Ohanessian, with the assistance of Carol K. Kreidler and Julia Sableski. Washington, D. C., Center for Applied Linguistics, 1964-

——————————— ———————————. Supplement, 1964-68. Washington, Center for Applied Linguistics [c1969]

Comprehensive and annotated bibliography covering materials published between the years 1953-63; in two parts. Pt. 1. deals with teaching materials for specific language backgrounds and with those for specialized fields. Includes section on dictionaries and on tests and examinations. Pt. 2 is a bibliography of monographs and periodical articles covering: linguistic background, methodology, preparation and analysis of materials, preparation of teachers, language testing and programs in specific geographical areas. Includes considerable amount of "classics" in the field of linguistics. Index. The supplement covers both areas bringing the first two parts up to date. It contains a section on contrastive studies of English and other languages, and one on teaching aids, categories omitted in the first two volumes. Index. *Use:* Although intended for teachers of English as a second language, it may be very useful to researchers in linguistics and to students.

22 Ollmann, Mary J., ed. *MLA Selective List of Materials: for use by teachers of modern foreign languages in elementary and secondary schools.* [New York] Modern Language Association of America, 1962. 162 p.

Lists 1850 items grouped by language and type of material. Covers: books, periodicals, films, filmstrips, discs, tape recordings and slides. Includes a general section, "All languages", applicable to study and teaching of any language and linguistics, giving annotated entries for bibliographies, dictionaries, basic texts, journals, pictures, reports, and pamphlets on language laboratory. Contains appendixes on criteria for evaluation of teaching aids and a directory of suppliers.

23 Pietrzyk, Alfred, Janet Roberts Duckett and Kathleen Pearce Lewis, eds. *Selected Titles in Sociolinguistics; An Annotated Preliminary Bibliography of Works on Multilingualism.*

Language Standardization: and Languages of Wider Communication. Washington, D. C., Center for Applied Linguistics of the Modern Language Association of America, 1964. 192. p.

Bibliography of books and periodical articles (the latter in the majority) containing over 700 entries and focusing on sociolinguistic studies of multilingualism, language standardization, including language policies, and languages of wider communication. An introductory section on general works is also provided. Indexes. *Use:* For instructors and students of linguistics and social sciences.

Rice, Frank A. and Allene Guss, eds. *Information Sources in Linguistics; A Bibliographical Handbook.* [Washington] Center for Applied Linguistics, 1965. 42 p.   **24**

A selective, partially annotated bibliography, meant "for the student of linguistics at the upper undergraduate or graduate level". – Introd. Subject arrangement; author index.

Robinson, Janet O., comp. *An Annotated Bibliography of Modern Language Teaching; books and articles 1946-1967.* London, Oxford University Press, 1969. 231 p. (Language and language learning, 23)   **25**

Contains some 1,500 entries, covering all aspects of modern language teaching. International in scope, it deals with the teaching of French, German, Italian, Russian and Spanish, including studies of each language based on modern linguistic theory. Focuses on educational problems related to teaching and learning English as a foreign or second language in Great Britain. Includes topics of general interest to all linguists: indexing and abstracting services, bibliographies, linguistics and its application to language teaching, value of contrastive studies, psycholinguistics, communication and teaching aids (radio, television, films, AV equipment, etc.). Indexes. *Use:* For teachers, librarians, students of language and linguistics in upper level courses, and for textbook writers.

Rutherford, Phillip R. *A Bibliography of American Doctoral Dissertations in Linguistics, 1900-1964.* [Washington] Center for Applied Linguistics, 1968. 139 p.   **26**

Contains over 1,700 entries giving authors' names, titles of dissertations, names of universities and dates of degrees granted by them. Index. *Use:* Intended to assist scholars with information on research that has been completed in the field of linguistics.

Scheurweghs, Gustave. *Analytical Bibliography of Writings on*
27 *Modern English Morphology and Syntax, 1877-1960.* Louvain, Belgium, Nauwelaerts, 1963-68. 4 vols. (Publication of the University of Louvain)

Contents. -v. 1. Periodical literature and miscellanies of the United States of America and Western and Northern Europe. With an appendix of Japanese publications by Hideo Yamaguchi (Fukui, Japan). -v. 2. Studies in bookform, including disserations and Programmabhandlungen published in the United States of America and Western and Northern Europe. With appendixes on Japanese publications by Hideo Yamaguchi, and on Czechoslovak publications by Ján Šimko (Bratislava). -v. 3. Soviet research on English morphology and syntax [by] G. G. Pocheptsov. English studies in Bulgaria, Poland, Rumania and Yugoslavia [by] M. Mincoff, A. Reszkiewicz, L. Levitchi, R. Filipović. -v. 4. Addenda and general indexes [by] G. Scheurweghs, continued by E. Vorlat. With a few addenda by Ján Šimko (Bratislava).

Shaughnessy, Amy E., ed. *Dissertation in Linguistics: 1957-64.*
28 [Washington, D. C.] Center for Applied Linguistics, 1965. 28 p.

Lists 373 doctoral dissertation titles, giving authors' names, dissertation titles, names of universities granting degrees, and dates. Includes topical and analytical index. The aim of this work, compiled mainly from data accessible to the Center by the Office of Scientific Personnel of the National Academy of Sciences–National Research Council, was to provide readily available information on all American Ph.D. theses in linguistics.

Shen, Yao and Ruth H. Crymes. *Teaching English as a Second*
29 *Language: A Classified Bibliography.* Honolulu, East-West Center Press [c1965] 110 p.

Contains 874 entries grouped under the headings: phonology, grammar, and methodology, plus a section on journals, with a sub-arrangement by country; not annotated. Index.

12

U. S. Information Agency. English Teaching Division. *Language.*
Washington, 1969. 61 p. (U. S. Information Agency. Subject   **30**
bibliography no. 3/69)

Intended primarily as an aid to teachers of linguistics, this is a
very useful annotated bibliography of books, collections of
articles and conference reports covering general linguistic
theory, its relation to other disciplines, and methodology of
language teaching. Emphasizes teaching of English as a
foreign language. Contains 172 entries, including contrastive
studies of English and Spanish, Italian and German. Provides
instructions for ordering books listed in the bibliography.

Walford, Albert J. *A Guide to Foreign Language Grammars and
Dictionaries.* 2d ed., rev. & enl. London, Library Association,   **31**
1967. 240 p.

An annotated selective "list of grammars, dictionaries and
audio-visual aids for the major foreign languages of Western
Europe plus Russian and Chinese. It is intended for teachers,
students, graduates who may be taking up a particular
language for the first time, scientists (for acquiring a reading
knowledge of a language on a minimum of grammar),
tourists, and librarians (for book selection and stock revision)." — Introd. Includes an author-title-subject index.

Walters, Theodore W. *The Georgetown Bibliography of Studies
Contributing to the Psycholinguistics of Language Learning.*   **32**
Washington, University of Georgetown Press [1965] 125 p.

A very useful bibliography of books, theses and periodical
articles, amounting to nearly thirteen hundred entries, all
arranged alphabetically. Includes topical index, subdivided
and arranged alphabetically within.

33   Modern Humanities Research Association. *Annual Bibliography of English Language and Literature.* Cambridge, University Press. v. 1, 1920- .

> Excellent publication devoted to English and American literature (arranged chronologically) and language (arranged by subject). Lists monographs and periodical articles; gives references to reviews of materials listed. Indexes.

34   *Bibliographic Index.* New York, H. W. Wilson. v. 1, 1937- .

> Semiannual; prior to 1951 quarterly, with annual and four- to five-year cumulations. Arranged alphabetically by subject. Lists separately published English and foreign bibliographies, bibliographies appended to books and those included in about 1,600 periodicals. Works on the subject of linguistics are listed under the headings *Language and languages* and *Linguistics*, with further alphabetical subdivisions.

35   *British Humanities Index.* London, Library Association. 1962- . Formerly *Subject Index to Periodicals.* Quarterly, with annual cumulations.

> Quarterly issues are by subject only, annuals by subject and by author (two sections). Indexes over 360 periodicals published in the United Kingdom. Covers a great deal of material on various aspects of language and linguistics.

36   Ottawa. National Library. *Canadian Theses;* a list of theses accepted by Canadian universities. Thèses canadiennes. 1952-

> An annual bibliography of theses, arranged by subject, then by university. Provides information on the unpublished typewritten manuscripts deposited with the institution granting the degree. Includes a section on linguistics, giving: author, title, degree and date. Contains author index and statistical tables of theses by university and by subject.

37   *Computer Abstracts.* St. Helier, Jersey, British Channel Islands. v. 1, 1957- . Monthly. Published by Technical Information Company.

Designed to provide a systematic guide to current computer literature, the abstracts cover four types of items: articles and papers in periodicals, conference proceedings, etc; U. S. government research reports; patents; books. Abstracts of the first three types are arranged in the above order within each classified section; book abstracts appear in a final part. Applications of computers are in a special section subdivided into specific area of application, including linguistics. Contains subject, author and patent indexes. Carries a supplement: *Computer News.*

Computing Reviews. New York. v. 1, 1960- .

Bi-monthly publication of the Association for Computing **38**
Machinery. "Aims to furnish computer-oriented persons in mathematics, engineering, the natural and social sciences, the humanities and other areas with critical information about all current publications in any area of the computer sciences. It is hoped thereby to further the development of computer sciences as a discipline, as an art, and as a tool for revolutionizing both our technology and our patterns of thinking."—Edit. Contains reviews and abstracts of books, articles, papers presented at conferences, theses, government publications, films, etc., arranged into several sections with further subdivisions. The section on applications of computers in humanities includes data on language translation and linguistics and on literature. Author index; cumulative indexes. Indexed in *Mathematical Reviews.*

Dissertation Abstracts. Ann Arbor, Mich., University Microfilms.
v. 1, 1938- . v. 1-11 issued as MICROFILM ABSTRACTS. **39**
Beginning with vol. 27, 1966 issued in two separate sections:

Dissertation Abstracts A The Humanities and Social Sciences and
Dissertation Abstracts B The Sciences and Engineering

Recent subtitle: "Abstracts of dissertations available on microfilm or as xerographic reproductions". A monthly compilation of abstracts of doctoral dissertations submitted to University Microfilms by more than 210 co-operating institutions (in 1969). Author and subject indexes for both sections are included in each part and all entries supplied with A or B symbols. Cumulative index at the end of each volume. Section A contains chapter "Language and literature". Indexed in *Annual Bibliography of English Language and Literature* and in *MLA International Bibliography*.

40 *Doctoral Dissertations Accepted by American Universities*. New York, H. W. Wilson. v. 1, 1933- v. 22, 1955.

Ceased publication with vol. 22. Superseded by *Index to American Doctoral Dissertations*, issued annually as No. 13 of each volume of Dissertation Abstracts. Arranged by subject, with subdivisions by university, it lists American and Canadian dissertations, giving author and title. Includes author and subject indexes.

41 *Education Index*. New York. v. 1, 1929-

"A cumulative subject index to a selected list of educational periodicals, proceedings and yearbooks", published monthly (Sept.–June) with annual cumulations by H. W. Wilson Co. Although concerned mainly with education, in all aspects and at all levels, it covers many topics of general interest in the field of. language and linguistics. Includes mathematical linguistics, psycholinguistics, sociolinguistics and related areas.

42 ASLIB. *Index to Theses Accepted for Higher Degrees in the Universities of Great Britain and Ireland*. v. 1- 1950/51- . London.

Annual publication of the Association of Special Libraries and Information Bureaux. Arranged by subject, with further subdivisions within. Under subject headings it lists: author, university, title, and degree. Includes section: "Language and literature". Author index. Editorial note to each volume provides information on loan privileges.

43 *Language and Language Behavior Abstracts*. Ann Arbor, Mich. v. 1, 1967- .

Quarterly publication of the Center for Research on Language & Language Behavior, University of Michigan, with the assistance of UNESCO. Computer processed, it contains abstracts of articles on linguistic, psychological and educa-

16

tional research relevant to language learning. Over a thousand journals in more than twenty languages are screened for LLBA; English at Ann Arbor, others in Paris. Indexes.

Language Teaching Abstracts. London. v. 1, 1968- .   44

Quarterly. Edited by the English-Teaching Information Centre of the British Council and the Centre for Information on Language Teaching, and published by Cambridge University Press. Meant as a primary source of information on latest research in modern languages, including English as a second language. Contains abstracts of articles appearing in some three hundred journals and covering general and applied linguistics, psychology of language learning, and theory and methods of education. Carries book reviews. Language-Teaching Abstracts incorporates the former English-Teaching Abstracts, published by the English-Teaching Information Centre from 1961 to 1967.

Linguistic Bibliography. Permanent International Committee of Linguists. Utrecht, 1939- .   45

French title page, *Bibliographie Linguistique*, also included. Annual. The years 1939-47 are covered in two volumes. International in scope, it lists book reviews and periodical articles on the subject of linguistics published in all major areas of the world. Includes monographs, serials, theses and essays arranged by the topic, e.g. General linguistics, with further subdivisions: Indo-European, Finno-Ugrian, etc. Author index.

MLA International Bibliography. New York. 1921- .   46

Published annually as supplements to P. M. L. A. (Publications of the Modern Language Association of America.) Known from 1921 to 1955 as *American Bibliography*, it expanded its coverage and changed the title to *Annual Bibliography* in 1956-62. In 1963 the title changed to *MLA International Bibliography*. Covers monographs and periodical articles from about 1,500 serial titles devoted to modern languages and literatures. Arranged by language families and chronologically subdivided. Author index. Beginning with 1970, *MLA International Bibliography* appears in a new multi-volume format, separate from PMLA. Volume Three of the set is devoted to linguistics. Published (in 1970) by the Pennsylvania State University Press as a special issue of the journal *General linguistics*, it is intended to so appear in subsequent years.

47 *Psychological Abstracts.* Lancaster, Pa. v. 1, 1927-.

Monthly publication of the American Psychological Association, it is an important bibliography of books and articles, containing sections on language and communication, psycholinguistics, speech and verbal behavior. Author index in each issue, author and detailed subject indexes in each volume; cumulated index for 1927-1959.

48 *Social Sciences & Humanities Index.* New York, H. W. Wilson. v. 19, 1966- .

Continues *International Index to Periodicals* with v. 19, 1966. Quarterly, with annual cumulations. An author and subject index covering over two hundred scholarly journals (mainly American and British; few Canadian) in the humanities and social sciences. Covers many aspects of language and linguistics.

49 *Year's Work in Modern Language Studies.* Edited for the Modern Humanities Research Association. Oxford, University Press. v. 1, 1930- .

Annual. The years 1940-49 are covered in one volume (v. 11). Contents grouped under the headings: Medieval Latin, Romance languages, Germanic languages, and Slavonic languages, is further divided into language and literature sections with chronological sub-arrangements. Includes descriptive and evaluative comments. Indexes. Indexed in *British Humanities Index*, also in *MLA International Bibliography*.

abbreviations, foreign terms and phrases, and idiomatic expressions. Supplemented by lists of signs and symbols; weights and measures; directory of colleges and universities; concise French, Spanish, Italian and German dictionaries; manual of style; historical dates; illustrations, maps; and other types of information. Convenient to use, this one-volume popular dictionary includes recent scientific and technological terms and provides numerous cross-references. Selected bibliography.

Webster's New International Dictionary of the English Language. 2d ed., unabridged [. . .] A. Merriam-Webster. William Allan   **58** Neilson, editor in chief, Thomas A. Knott, general editor [and] Paul W. Carhart, managing editor. Springfield, Mass., G. & C. Merriam Co., 1937 [c1934] 2 vols.

The oldest and most famous American dictionary; first published in 1828, revised in later editions (1909, 1934). It is a general purpose dictionary, with no bias and no specialization. Claims to contain 600,000 entries. Gives definitions in historical sequence. Provides tables of abbreviations; symbols; pronouncing gazetteer; and a pronouncing biographical dictionary.

Webster's Third New International Dictionary of the English Language unabridged [. . .] Ed. in chief Philip Babcock Gove,   **59** and the Merriam-Webster Editorial Staff. Springfield, Mass., G. & C. Merriam, 1967 [c1966] 2,662 p.

One of the most controversial reference sources of the past decade, first published in 1961. Contains 450,000 entries, of which 100,000 were new words introduced by new developments in science and technology. Gives brief and precise definitions. Concentrates on contemporary rather than historical usage. Good for etymologies, synonyms, foreign words and phrases, and slang expressions. Omits biographical and geographical material, and words obsolete before 1755. Gives pronunciation as used in "general cultivated conversational usage"; indicates regional variations. Includes some 200,000 quotations. *Use:* For general reader and scholar alike.

Murray, Sir James A. H., ed. *The Oxford English Dictionary*; being a corrected re-issue with an introduction, supplement, and bibliography of *A new English dictionary on historical principles,* founded mainly on the materials collected by The Philological Society and ed. by James A. H. Murray, Henry Bradley, W. A. Craigie, C. T. Onions. Oxford, Clarendon Press [1961, c1933] 13 vols.

60

Began in 1884 and completed 1928, it had no revisions since 1933. Covers literary periods from Chaucer to recent times; excludes words obsolete before 1150. Gives pronunciation and history of every word included, from the date it was introduced to the language; indicates the use and meaning at different periods. Includes synonyms, foreign words, and slang expressions. Omits biographical and geographical material. Contains numerous quotations. Supplement (v.13) includes 26,000 new words in use between 1884–1933. *Use:* Most exhaustive English language dictionary; for scholars and students concerned with historical aspects of the language.

[Murray, Sir James A. H.] *The Shorter English Oxford Dictionary on Historical Principles.* Prepared by William Little . . . H. W. Fowler . . . J. Coulson . . . Revised and edited by C. T. Onions . . . 3d. ed. rev. with addenda. Oxford, The Clarendon Press [1965] 2 vols.

61

First published in 1933. Excellent British dictionary based on the great Oxford English Dictionary. Provides the same type of information, giving definitions in order of historical development, and omitting biographical and geographical data, but contains less quotations and etymologies. Indicates pronunciation using International Phonetic Alphabet.

Onions, Charles T., ed. *The Oxford Dictionary of English Etymology.* Ed. by C. T. Onions, with the assistance of G. W. S. Friedrichsen and R. W. Burchfield. Oxford, Clarendon Press [c1966] 1,025 p.

62

A comprehensive, scholarly work, containing about 38,000 entries. Gives pronunciation, explanation, origin, and chronologically arranged meanings. Does not include latest scientific and technological terminology.

22

Partridge, Eric. *Origins; a short etymological dictionary of modern English.* New York, Macmillan, 1966. 972 p.   **63**

> First published in 1958. Contains over 10,000 commonly used words; only a small number of scientific and technological terms, and a few examples of slang. Includes a list of prefixes, suffixes, and compound-forming elements.

Skeat, Walter W. *An Etymological Dictionary of the English Language.* New ed., rev. and enl. Oxford, Clarendon Press [1963, 1910] 780 p.   **64**

> A classic in the field of etymological dictionaries, this scholarly work covers over 14,000 entries, giving numerous references to a variety of multi-lingual sources. Includes notes on languages cited in the dictionary, canons for etymology, bibliography of books consulted, and appendixes containing lists of prefixes, suffices, homonyms, doublets, Indogermanic roots, and distribution of words according to the languages from which they are derived.

Historical

Bosworth, Joseph. *An Anglo-Saxon Dictionary* based on the manuscript collections of the late Joseph Bosworth . . . Edited and enlarged by T. Northcotte Toller . . . [London] Oxford University Press [1964, c1898] 1,302 p.   **65**

> ——————— ——————. Supplement, by T. Northcotte Toller . . . [London] Oxford University Press [1955, 1921] 768 p.

> An invaluable source of information, with numerous quotations and precise references to original works. Supplement includes revision and enlargement of letters A to G.

Kurath, Hans and Sherman M. Kuhn, eds. *Middle English Dictionary.* Ann Arbor, University of Michigan Press [c1956- .(In progress)]   **66**

> Important work, conducted as a special project of the University of Michigan, intending to cover individual histories of words in the English language from 1100 to 1475. Provides numerous quotations arranged chronologically.

67 Mathews, Mitford, ed. *A Dictionary of Americanisms on Historical Principles.* Chicago, University of Chicago Press [1951] 1,946 p.

> A dictionary of exclusively American contributions to the English language, listing words and phrases first noted in the United States; words having unique American meaning; and those made by combining older forms. Gives earliest meaning first. Includes slang expressions. Contains numerous quotations from books, newspapers, magazines, mail-order catalogs and other sources. Indicates pronunciation using International Phonetic Alphabet.

68 Nares, Robert. *A Glossary of Words, Phrases, Names and Allusions in the Works of English Authors, Particularly of Shakespeare and his Contemporaries.* New ed., with considerable additions both of words and examples, by J. O. Halliwell and Thomas Wright. London, Routledge; New York, Dutton, 1905. Detroit, Reprinted by Gale Research Co., 1966. 981 p.

> Includes numerous quotations.

69 Shipley, Joseph T. *Dictionary of Early English.* With a preface by Mark Van Doren. New York, Philosophical Library [1955] 753 p. (Midcentury reference library)

> Covers roughly ten centuries, from the 8th to the 18th. Includes: words found in literary works of Chaucer, Spencer, Shakespeare, Chatterton, Ossian, Scott and other outstanding authors; words that belong to the history of early England, describing social, political, and economic conditions; works of special interest in meaning, background or associated folklore, and other rare words not used currently.

70 Thornton, Richard H. *An American Glossary*; being an attempt to illustrate certain Americanisms upon historical principles. New York, Ungar [1962] 3 vols.

> V. 3: Supplement, edited by Louise Hanley, compiled from material published posthumously in *Dialect Notes*, v. 6.

> Originally published in London in 1912, this is a scholarly work considered an indispensable supplement to the Oxford English Dictionary. Contains 14,000 chronologically arranged

quotations from books, newspapers, magazines, pamphlets and congressional debates, following definition of each word in the dictionary.

Includes: forms of speech now obsolete or provincial in England which survived in the U. S.; words and phrases of distinctly American origin; nouns which indicate quadrupeds, birds, trees, articles of food distinctively American; names and classes of persons; words which have assumed a new meaning; and words and phrases found earlier in American than English writers.

Wright, Thomas. *A Dictionary of Obsolete and Provincial English*, containing words from the English writers previous to the 71 nineteenth century which are no longer in use, or are not used in the same sense. And words which are now used only in the provincial dialect. Detroit, Gale Research Co., 1967. 2 vols.

First published in England in 1857.

Pronouncing

Jones, Daniel. *Everyman's English Pronouncing Dictionary*; containing over 58,000 words in International Phonetic Transcription. 12th ed. [rev.] London, J. M. Dent [1964, i.e. 1963] 539 p. (Everyman's reference library)

Records colloquial speech of the educated Southern British English. Gives words, including some proper names, in the symbols of the International Phonetic Association. Contains no definitions. Includes a brief bibliography of books on English pronunciation, and a glossary of phonetic terms. *Use:* For students, teachers, foreigners, and all concerned with correct British pronunciation.

Kenyon, John Samuel and Thomas Albert Knott. *A Pronouncing Dictionary of American English*. Springfield, Mass., G. & C. 73 Merriam [c1953] 484 p.

The counterpart of Daniel Jones's *English Pronouncing Dictionary*, dealing with Southern British English, this guide to modern American speech presents "the pronunciation of cultivated colloquial English in the United States". Specifies regional differences. Gives many proper, historical and literary names. Contains no definitions. Indicates pronunciation utilizing the International Phonetic Alphabet. *Use:* A general-purpose handbook intended for students, teachers, editors, and all interested in correct speech.

Semantic frequency

74 West, Michael. *A General Service List of English Words*, with semantic frequencies and a supplementary word-list for the writing of popular science and technology. [Rev. and enl. ed.] London, Longmans, Green [1953] 588 p.

First published in 1936 under the title *Interim Report on Vocabulary Selection*, this is a revised version of a study on basic vocabulary for learning English as a foreign language. Shows frequency of occurrence of various meanings and uses of words found in a five million word count. *Use:* Intended for teachers and textbook writers, it is an important and interesting work recommended for students concerned with semantics and literary style.

Slang

75 Partridge, Eric. *A Dictionary of Slang and Unconventional English*; colloquialisms and catch-phrases, solecisms and catachreses, nicknames, vulgarisms and such Americanisms as have been naturalized. [5th ed. Suppl. much enl.] New York, Macmillan, 1966 [i.e. 1961] 1,362 p.

76 Partridge, Eric. *A Dictionary of the Underworld*; British & American, being the vocabularies of crooks, criminals, racketeers, beggars and tramps, convicts, the commercial underword, the drug traffic, the white slave traffic, spivs. London, Routledge & K. Paul [1964, 1949] 817 p.

77 Wenthworth, Harold and Stuart Berg Flexner, eds. *Dictionary of American Slang*. With a supplement by Stuart Berg Flexner. New York, Crowell [c1967] 718 p.

Includes extensive bibliography. First published in 1960, this dictionary is kept up to date by the supplement. Covers thousands of slang definitions, including derogatory and taboo words. Introductory notes and appendixes provide for analysis of linguistic processes involved into the making of new slang expressions.

Synonyms & antonyms

Buck, Carl D. *A Dictionary of Selected Synonyms in the Principal Indo-European Languages; a contribution to the history of ideas.* University of Chicago Press [1949] 1,515 p.　　**78**

Classified by semantic groups (e.g. time), it lists synonyms under each entry (e.g. age, day), and gives the equivalent word in some 30 languages. Provides etymology and semantic history of each term.

Hayakawa, Samuel I. *Funk & Wagnalls Modern Guide to Synonyms and Related Words*; lists of antonyms, copious cross-references, a complete and legible index [by] S. I. Hayakawa and the Funk and Wagnalls dictionary staff. New York, Funk & Wagnalls [1968] 726 p.　　**79**

Arranged by key words, with index, this is a good standard guide to synonyms, giving current meaning of some 6,000 commonly used words. Contains over 1,000 essays supplied with cross-references, and antonyms. Concentrates on clear and precise definitions of standard terms as used by educated people, dealing little with etymology and history of the words. Includes only a few slang expressions.

Roget's International Thesaurus. 3d. ed. New York, Crowell [c1962] 1,528 p.　　**80**

A dictionary of words grouped by ideas, with an alphabetical word index referring to the specific category. Contains 240,000 terms. Includes scientific and technological vocabulary; synonyms, antonyms, colloquialisms and slang expressions. *Use:* Essential to professional writers, speakers and translators; recommended to all students working on term papers.

81 *Webster's Dictionary of Synonyms*; a dictionary of discriminated synonyms with antonyms and analogous and contrasted words. 1st ed. Springfield, Mass., Merriam [1951] 907 p.

One of the most popular comprehensive dictionaries of synonyms, supplied with numerous quotations from literary sources, classical and modern. Contains extensive introductory notes including a survey of the history of English synonymy.

ENCYCLOPEDIA OF LINGUISTICS

82 Meetham, A. R. *Encyclopaedia of Linguistics, Information and Control.* Editor-in-chief: A. R. Meetham. Associate editor: R. A. Hudson. [1st ed.] Oxford, New York, Pergamon Press [1969] 718 p.

An interdisciplinary encyclopedia aiming "to help human communications in the wide area which is being opened up by computers and by the new thinking they have generated"—Foreword. Contains articles contributed by physicists, mathematicians, computer scientists, system consultants, economists, psychologists, physiologists, documentalists and students of linguistics. All articles are supplied with cross-references and followed by bibliographies. Included is an extensive index/glossary of terms; the International Phonetic Alphabet; and a list of associations between articles on the end papers.

THEORY AND PHILOSOPHY OF LANGUAGE AND METHODOLOGY OF LINGUISTICS

Allen, Harold B., ed. *Readings in Applied English Linguistics.* 2d ed. New York, Appleton-Century-Crofts [c1964] 535 p.   **83**

Collection of articles meant as a source book for teachers of English. It is "intended to meet the need for representation of current linguistic thought and applications" . . . —Pref. Deals with the following topics: historical background, English linguistics today, linguistic geography, linguistics and usage, linguistics and the teaching of grammar and composition, etc. *Use:* Helpful source of reference to teachers of English from elementary schools to graduate seminars.

Anderson, Wallace L. & Norman C. Stageberg, eds. *Introductory Readings on Language.* Rev. ed. New York, Holt, Rinehart and Winston [1966] 551 p.   **84**

Aims to present basic information about language. Includes forty-two essays, dealing with various linguistic topics of current interest. Grouped in ten sections the articles discuss: the nature of language; language history; words; forms and meanings; semantics; language and literature; the sounds of language; usage; linguistic geography; structural and transformational grammar; clear thinking. Supplied with suggested assignments, and lists of further readings. Indexes. *Use:* Intended as a text for freshman English; recommended to all students in undergraduate English courses.

Bach, Emmon and Robert T. Harms, eds. *Universals in Linguistic Theory.* New York, Holt, Rinehart and Winston [1968] 210 p.   **85**

A collection of four papers presented at a University of Texas (Austin) symposium, in 1967, concerned with questions of general linguistic theory—"universals". Contains: "The case for case", by C. J. Fillmore; "Nouns and noun phrases", by Emmon Bach; "The role of semantics in a grammar", by J. D. McCawley; "Linguistic universals and linguistic change", by Paul Kiparsky. The first three papers discuss mainly syntax and semantics; the last deals with phonology. Included is a list of bibliographical references. *Use:* For all concerned with developments in current linguistic theories.

86 Bazell, Charles E., ed. *In Memory of J. R. Firth.* London, Longmans, 1966. 500 p. (Longmans' linguistics library)

A collection of twenty-seven essays dedicated to the memory of John Firth by his scholarly associates. Deals with various aspects of contemporary linguistics, some of which present continuation of Firth's own theories of language. Includes a bibliography of Firth's writings. *Use:* For all students of linguistics.

87 Bloomfield, Leonard. *Language.* New York, Holt, Rinehart and Winston [c1933] 564 p.

Although meant by the author "for the general reader" the book is de facto directed to the linguists. It is now considered classic of modern structural linguistics. Discussed here are all important aspects of the subject, including history of linguistic study, phonetic structure of language, together with a short survey of the languages of the world; functions of speech and semantic changes as well as phonetic and grammatical analogies in other languages. Included are chapters on language study and teaching. Contains excellent bibliographies, notes, short table of phonetic symbols and index.

88 Bolinger, Dwight. *Aspects of Language.* New York, Harcourt, Brace & World [c1968] 326 p.

Written in a clear simple language, this book aims to explain, and not to teach, the essence of modern linguistics in all its aspects. Contains fourteen chapters, each followed by "Additional remarks and applications". Index. *Use:* For general readers and students.

89 Bolton, Whitney F., ed. *The English Language.* Cambridge [Eng.] Cambridge University Press, 1966-1969. 2 vols.

Contents: v. 1. Essays by English and American men of letters, 1490-1839. -v. 2. Essays by linguists and men of letters, 1858-1964. Selections of forty-two essays (twenty in volume 1, and twenty-two in volume 2), covering a variety of topics, and illustrating both the internal and the external history of literary English prose since the end of the 15th century to our times. The essays represent the development and changes in the study of English language revealing the growing importance of linguistic resources and linguistic theory for literary style, and show the influence of literary men on linguistic opinion; the adoption of literary English as the premier dialect of the language; and the dependence of the literary dialect on the resources of English in each age. Included are study questions and select indexes of literary and linguistic topics. *Use:* For all students of English language and linguistics; for linguists, literary historians, teachers of language and speech, and all concerned with literary style.

Carnap, Rudolf. *The Logical Syntax of Language.* London, Routledge & K. Paul [1964] 352 p. (International library of psychology, philosophy and scientific method) **90**

"Translated by Amethe Smeaton." First published in German as *Logische Syntax der Sprache*, in 1934; published in English translation in 1937.

Aims to give a systematic exposition of the method of "logical syntax" which uses symbols instead of words. Deals with symbolic languages only but states that the syntactical concepts and rules may—in their general character—be also applied to the analysis of the complicated word languages. Contains bibliographies and indexes. *Use:* For students of linguistics, logic and philosophy, concerned with syntax of languages beyond introductory level.

Cassirer, Ernst. *The Philosophy of Symbolic Forms.* Translated by Ralph Manheim; preface and introduction by Charles W. Hendel. New Haven, Yale University Press, 1953-57. 3 vols. [v. 1. Language. (1953)] **91**

Originally published in German, in 1923, this important work consists of three volumes. First, essential to linguistic science, has a subtitle *The phenomenology of linguistic form* and deals with: the problem of language in the history of philosophy; language in the phase of sensuous expression (sign and sound); language in the phase of intuitive expression (space and spatial relations, time, concept of number, "inner intuition"); language as expression of conceptual thought (concept and class information in language); language and the expression of the forms of pure relation (judgment and the concepts of relation). Indexes. *Use:* For those studying history of linguistics and philosophy; not for laymen.

92 Chao, Yuen Ren. *Language and Symbolic Systems.* Cambridge, University Press, 1968. 240 p.

An interesting introductory book dealing broadly with the whole field of language and linguistics. Discusses the relationship between language and culture, emphasizing the symbolic systems in language, writing and various aspects of modern communication technology. Draws many examples from Chinese linguistics. Includes a bibliography, an index, tables and diagrams. *Use:* Written in a lucid, very readable style, it is recommended to general readers, linguistic experts and laymen alike.

93 Dixon, Robert M. *Linguistic Science and Logic.* The Hague, Mouton, 1963. 108 p. (Janua linguarum. Series minor, nr. 28)

The author states that his writings belong with the neo-Firthian linguistics and the "British school". Aims "to present a unified picture of a particular approach" (Edinburgh) where linguistic science must fit into a more general philosophical attitude, and grammar be considered in relation to a complete theory of linguistics. Discusses scientific nature of linguistics, the school of Chomsky, and the relationship between linguistics and a theory of "descriptive logic". *Use:* For linguists and logicians.

94 Ebeling, C. L. *Linguistic Units.* 's-Gravenhage, Mouton, 1962 [c1959] 143 p. (Janua linguarum. Studia memoriae Nicolai Van Wijk dedicata, nr. 12)

Aims to define precise criteria for identifying linguistic units: the phoneme (unit of sound), the valence (unit of meaning), and the morpheme (unit of sound and meaning). It also deals with the theories of outstanding linguists, especially Bloomfield, Jakobson, Hjelmslev, Martinet, Twadell and Hockett. *Use:* For students in advanced linguistics courses only.

95 Firth, John R. *Papers in Linguistics, 1934-1951.* London, New York, Oxford University Press [1957, reprinted 1964] 233 p.

A selection of papers from the work of the first professor of general linguistics in the U. K., which appeared over a period of more than twenty-five years. Included are essays on various aspects of phonetics, semantics, technique of linguistic analysis, and descriptive grammar. Since the author was on the staff of the School of Oriental and African Studies, University of London (1944-56), many examples are drawn from the Far Eastern languages, especially Chinese, Japanese and Indian languages. Contains a "Bibliography of other works based on similar principles and methods." Index. *Use:* Interesting book to "nontechnical" readers and to specialists in the field alike. However, due to outstanding progress in linguistics during recent years, it has mainly a historical value. It presents the views of the leading English linguist.

Firth, John R. *The Tongues of Men, and Speech.* London, Oxford University Press, 1964. 211 p. (Language and language learning, 2) **96**

First published in 1930's, these are two important introductory works to the Firth's theory of language and to recent trends in British linguistics. *Use:* For students of general linguistics at all levels.

Fodor, Jerry A. and Jerrold J. Katz. *The Structure of Language; Readings in the Philosophy of Language.* Englewood Cliffs, N. J., Prentice-Hall [1964] 612 p. **97**

A collection of papers by linguists, arranged in groups under: linguistic theory, grammar, extensions of grammar, semantics, psychological implications. Stress is put on the philosophy of language. *Use:* "A text for courses in the philosophy of language at the advanced undergraduate and graduate levels . . . "–Pref.

Gleason, Henry A. *An Introduction to Descriptive Linguistics.* Rev. ed. New York, Holt, Rinehart & Winston [c1961] 503 p. **98**

First published in 1955. Popular course book meant for senior and graduate students. Deals with phonology, morphology, syntax, acoustic phonetics, dialectology, diachronic and geographic linguistics, writing systems and language classifications. Stress is put on synchronic descriptions. Historical matters are excluded. Contains index and excellent, partially annotated "selected bibliography." Supplemented by the *Workbook in Descriptive Linguistics* (N. Y., Holt, c1955; 88 pp.) including numerous exercises, particularly those for drill in phonetics. Both books can be used independently.

99 Gleason, Henry A., Jr. *Linguistics and English Grammar.* New York, Holt, Rinehart and Winston [1965] 519 p.

Intended as a guide book to English grammars, it aims to explain the inter-relations between linguistics and the grammar. Discusses historical background, topics in English syntax, including language structure and generative grammar, language variation, language comparison and literary style. Includes excellent annotated bibliography and index. *Use:* For teachers of English; recommended to all students concerned with linguistic description and analysis.

100 Gleason, Patrick and Nancy Wakefield, eds. *Language and Culture.* Columbus, Ohio, C. E. Merrill [1958] 200 p.

An important interdisciplinary anthology of essays presenting the relation between language and other fields: literature, philosophy, anthropology and sociology. Papers are grouped under two main headings: "Origins, limits, and general problems" and "The uses of language". Includes contributions by Sapir, Jespersen, Ullmann, Whorf, Cassirer, Hockett, George Orwell, and others. *Use:* For linguists, literary critics, philosophers, communication engineers, anthropologists and sociologists.

101 Godel, Robert, ed. *A Geneva School Reader in Linguistics.* Bloomington, Indiana University Press [c1969] 361 p. (Indiana University studies in the history and theory of linguistics)

Introduction by M. Mourelle-Lema. An important collection of papers written by the linguists of the Geneva School. Most of the lectures and articles presented here, in their original French version, have been published before but are not easily accessible elsewhere. Ferdinand de Saussure's notes from lectures which he delivered at the University of Geneva (ca 1894-95) appear in print for the first time. Included are works by Charles Bally, Albert Sechehaye, Serge Karcevski and others. The introductory chapter of the book presents, in English, a valuable bio-bibliographical record of the Saussurian School of Geneva. *Use:* Essential to all linguists.

Greenberg, Joseph H. *Essays in Linguistics.* Chicago, University of Chicago Press [1963, c1957] 108 p.   **102**

A collection of essays concerned with the methodology of language description, historical linguistics, and the relationship between language and culture. Contains a glossary of definitions and index. *Use:* For linguists, anthropologists, logicians and mathematicians.

Greenberg, Joseph H., ed. *Universals of Language*; report of a conference held at Dobbs Ferry, New York, April 13-15, 1961.   **103** 2d ed. Cambridge, Mass., MIT Press [1966] 337 p.

A collection of papers presented at the 1961 conference by the outstanding contemporary linguists, psychologists and anthropologists, discussing the question of generalizations about language, together with its phonological, semantic and historical aspects. Final topics, covered by Jakobson, Casagrande, and Osgood, deal with implications of language universals for linguistics, anthropology and psycholinguistics. Bibliography. Index. *Use:* For linguists, psychologists and anthropologists.

Hall, Robert A. *Introductory Linguistics.* [1st ed.] Philadelphia, Chilton Books [1964] 508 p.   **104**

The book is wide in scope but well organized into several parts with subdivisions into chapters; the latter amounting to eighty in all. Covers: description of language, linguistic geography, writing and language, linguistic change, linguistics and related fields, and the uses of linguistics. History of linguistics and a survey of world's languages are omitted. Includes bibliography, table of phonetic symbols and index. *Use:* Intended for use in two-semester college course, this is a readable, highly informative and a valuable book to teachers and instructors in linguistics.

Hall, Robert A., Jr. *Linguistics and Your Language.* 2nd rev. ed. of "Leave your Language Alone!" Garden City, N. Y.,   **105** Doubleday [1960, c1950] 265 p.

Addressed to the general public, this is "a brief, popular discussion of a number of problems connected with language, and of the science of language–linguistics–and what is can contribute to the solution of these problems."–Pref. Deals with use, structure, meaning, change and learning of a language. Two appendixes contain a short annotated bibliography and a list of phonetic symbols.

Hamp, Eric P., Fred W. Householder and Robert Austerlitz, eds. *Readings in Linguistics II.* Chicago, University of Chicago Press [1966] 395 p.

106

In English, French and German. Intended to follow the *Readings in Linguistics I,* edited by Martin Joos, in 1957, for the ACLS Committee on Language Programs. Meant as a handbook on linguistic theory and a textbook in the history of linguistics, it is a collection of scholarly articles representing European approaches to the field between the years of 1929-61. Attempt is made to give the full coverage of aspects the area offers. Includes often neglected branches of linguistics, e.g. graphemics. Excludes items easily available in print and articles too long for this volume. No index.

Harris, Zellig S. *Structural Linguistics.* Chicago, University of Chicago Press [1963, c1951] 384 p.

107

Formerly entitled *Methods in Structural Linguistics.* Discusses operations and elements of linguistics. "The research methods are arranged here in the form of the successive procedures of analysis imposed by the working linguist upon his data."–Introd. Includes author's "Preface for the fourth impression" describing developments of linguistic methods that took place since the book was first written. *Use:* Book intended for students of linguistics and those interested in the subject. "For those who use linguistic methods in research or teaching, the techniques are given (. . .) without employing the terminology of logic. For those who are primarily interested in the logic of distributional relations, which constitutes the basic method of structural linguistics, a minimum of knowledge about language and linguistics has been assumed here".–Pref.

Hill, Archibald A., ed. *Linguistics Today.* New York, Basic Books [c1969] 291 p.

108

An important collection of twenty-four essays, derived from lectures broadcast by the Voice of America in its Forum series, by prominent linguists, covering a variety of topics and points of view in their study of the present state of language science in the United States. Discussed subjects include: the nature and history of linguistics; phonology and phonetics; morphology and syntax; lexicology and semantics; history of language and the family of languages, dialects; language and communication; computational linguistics; machine translation; relations of linguistics with anthropology, psychology, literary criticism, language teaching, and the use of linguistic and paralinguistic analysis in psychiatric diagnosis. Separate chapters deal with well-known European and American schools of linguistics. The final section is the editor's summary and projection into the future. Index. *Use:* For linguists, students and teachers of English language and linguistics, literary historians and critics, psychologists, anthropologists, communication engineers and all others concerned with current trends in linguistics.

Henle, Paul, ed. *Language, Thought and Culture.* By Roger W. Brown [and others] Ann Arbor, University of Michigan Press **109** [1965] 273 p. (Ann Arbor paperbacks, AA97)

A collection of essays by leading linguists, anthropologists, literary critics, philosophers, psychologists and sociologists, aiming to contribute to an integrated study of language. Discussed topics are: language, thought, and culture; the growth of concepts; a stimulus-response analysis of language and meaning; artificial languages; some aspects of language; 'cognitive' and 'noncognitive'; metaphor; symbolism in the nonrepresentative arts; symbolism and the representative arts. Includes bibliographical notes to each chapter. *Use:* Recommended to students of language and linguistics at all levels and to those in the related fields; also to general interested readers.

Hjelmslev, Louis. *Prolegomena to a Theory of Language.* Translated by Francis J. Whitfield. [Rev. English ed.] Madison, **110** University of Wisconsin Press, 1963 [c1961] 144 p.

Originally published in Danish, 1943; first English ed. 1953. Divided into sections discussing three main points: the general criteria for a theory of language; the specific features of linguistic theory and the relationship of language to semiotic. Emphasis is on glossematics, the Hjelmslev's theory of an analysis of language whereby any linguistic item is defined by form and content. The aim of glossematics is to indicate the relationships (triads) of various parts of the linguistic analysis based on examples of different languages. Contains very useful chapter on definitions of linguistic terms in both English and Danish. Index.

111 Hockett, Charles F. *A Course in Modern Linguistics.* New York, Macmillan [1958] 621 p.

Comprehensive textbook dealing with all aspects of language. Includes chapters on linguistic prehistory. Interesting, written in a clear style devoid of too many technical terms. *Use:* Excellent source of information for all students of linguistics.

112 Hughes, John P. *The Science of Language; an introduction to linguistics.* New York, Random House [1962] 305 p.

Aims to present the fundamentals of all topics comprised by the science of linguistics. In a lucid style discusses definitions and historical development of major languages of the world; also deals with scientific description of language and linguistic analysis. Includes maps and diagrams. Contains extensive bibliography and indexes. *Use:* For both undergraduate and graduate students and instructors in language and linguistics, and for general readers.

113 Hymes, Dell, ed. *Language in Culture and Society; a reader in linguistics and anthropology.* New York, Harper & Row [1964] 764 p.

An important anthology of sixty-nine papers and selections from work of scholars, dealing with anthropological and social aspects of linguistics. Grouped in ten parts, the topics are: the scope of linguistic anthropology; equality, diversity, relativity; world view and grammatical categories; cultural focus and semantic field; role, socialization, and expressive speech; speech play and verbal art; social structure and speech community; processes and problems of change; relationships in time and space; and toward historical perspective. Included are: the editor's introduction and a reference note, preceding and following each section respectively, extensive general bibliography, index of references note in general bibliography, and index of language names. *Use:* Recommended to all concerned with language, linguistics, anthropology and sociology.

Jakobson, Roman. *Child Language, Aphasia and Phonological Universals.* The Hague, Mouton, 1968. 101 p. (Janua linguarum. Series minor, nr. 72)   **114**

Originally published as *Kindersprache* . . . in 1941, this is an important work on phonological typology and the related problems of language acquisition and phonemic regression. The importance of this classic monograph continues to grow through the years due to a formal linking of the problems of linguistic universals and of language acquisition, which have re-emerged as central problems in current thinking. Includes bibliography. *Use:* For students and researchers in linguistics, psychology and language pathology.

Jespersen, Otto. *Language: Its Nature, Development and Origin.* London, Allen & Unwin [1959, 1922] 448 p.   **115**

Surveys the history of linguistic science and discusses the linguistic development of the child, the individual and the world in relation to language changes in time. Deals also with origin and progress of speech and with that of grammatical elements. Contains index. *Use:* Written in a lucid style, and interesting, it is recommended to all concerned with the history of language and linguistics.

Jespersen, Otto. *The Philosophy of Grammar.* London, Allen & Unwin [1963, 1924] 359 p.   **116**

A presentation of the author's views of the general principles of grammar common to all languages, and based on direct observation of speech. Gives primary importance to "living speech", placing written and printed documents (ancient languages) secondary in the development of linguistic studies and setting up grammatical theories. Includes appendix and index. *Use:* Important to all students of linguistics and essential to instructors in grammar.

117 Jespersen, Otto. *Selected Writings.* London, Allen & Unwin [1962] 849 p.

A collection of thirty-four linguistic papers published to commemorate the hundredth anniversary of Jespersen's birth. The reprints, dated from 1894 to 1933, deal with English grammar, phonetics, history of English, language teaching, international language, and other topics. *Use:* For all concerned with English language and linguistics.

118 Joos, Martin, ed. *Readings in Linguistics I; the Development of Descriptive Linguistics in America 1925-56.* [Prepared for the Committee on Language Programs of the American Council of Learned Societies] 4th ed. Chicago, University of Chicago Press [1966, c1957] 421 p.

A companion volume to *Readings in Linguistics II*, edited by Eric P. Hamp, 1966. Contains reprints of forty-three articles by contemporary American linguists. Chronological arrangement of papers, from 1947 through 1956, is designed to show the development of descriptive linguistics. Excluded are only a few branches of linguistics: acoustic phonetics, perception theory, information theory, and the new trend in modern American linguistics known as transformational grammar. Includes "Comments on certain technical terms." No index. Useful for studies in the history of linguistics.

119 Katz, Jerrold J. *The Philosophy of Language.* New York, Harper & Row [1966] 326 p. (Studies in language)

Aims to develop a new approach to the philosophy of language, which the author considers separate from the philosophy of linguistics. Dwells on the twentieth century philosophy of language: logical empiricism and "ordinary language" philosophy. Discusses backgrounds of linguistic communication and description; concentrates on grammatical and semantic theories. Finally, demonstrates the application of his theory of language to solving sample philosophical problems. *Use:* For linguists, philosophers and students in advanced linguistic courses.

120 Keller, Joseph R. *Linguistic Theory and the Study of English; a selective outline.* Minneapolis, Burgess Pub. Co. [1968] 91 p.

Focuses upon selected general theories affecting the study of English: the theory of sound change, the theory of language as a structure, the generative-transformational theory of grammar, the formalist-structural theory of styles and the related problem of usage, the Sapir-Whorf theory of linguistic relativity, and the formalist theory of the hierarchical importance of poetics. Following each chapter are valuable, although very concise, lists of suggested readings and notes. *Use:* Recommended to all students of English language and linguistics beyond introductory level.

Kerr, Elizabeth M. and Ralph M. Aderman, eds. *Aspects of American English.* New York, Harcourt, Brace & World [1963] **121** 272 p. (Harbrace sourcebooks)

Aims to help students in the use of sourcebooks for teaching techniques of documentation, and in the study of American English lnaguage composition. Coordinates material on language with readings on modern fiction and drama, focusing on sentence structure, grammar, usage, and vocabulary. Presents selections of papers by outstanding contemporary linguists, dealing with principles of language, historical aspects, regional aspects, literary and colloquial aspects, and social or class aspects. Includes suggestions for brief papers or written reports after each section. Contains topics for longer papers, notes on the authors, and bibliography. *Use:* Recommended for instructors and all students of English language and linguistics, and for general readers.

Laird, Charlton and Robert M. Gorrell, eds. *English as Language: Backgrounds, Development, Usage.* New York, Harcourt, Brace **122** & World [1961] 279 p. (Harbrace sourcebooks)

A collection of papers designed for the study of English from about the year 1000 to the present time, tracing development and growth in the science of the language. Divided into sections discussing: language as it works, the language as it was, early observations on language, development of the dictionary, prescriptive grammar and usage problems, and the modern problem of usage. Each section is supplied with subjects for discussions, suggestions for investigation, reports, or brief papers. *Use:* For instructors and students in language and linguistics, especially for undergraduates.

Langacker, R. W. *Language and its Structure: Some Fundamental*
123   *Linguistic Concepts.* New York, Harcourt, Brace & World
[c1968] 260 p.

An excellent and concise introduction to the study of
language, it offers an up-to-date information on language
structure and linguistic relationships. Contains tables, diagrams, brief bibliography and index. *Use:* For all students of
linguistics and for general readers.

Langendoen, Donald T. *The London School of Linguistics: A*
124   *Study of the Linguistic Theories of B. Malinowski and J. R.*
Firth. Cambridge, Mass., MIT Press, 1968. 123 p. (MIT Press
research monograph, no. 46)

Shows the development of linguistics in the 20th century,
with focus on the London School and its contributions. Deals
with: the linguistic views of B. Malinowski; the early views of
J. R. Firth; the later views of J. R. Firth; and exemplifica-
tions of prosodic analysis. Contains bibliography and index.
Use: For linguists and others interested in the development
of linguistics in the 20th century.

Lenneberg, Eric H. *Biological Foundations of Language.* With
125   appendices by Noam Chomsky and Otto Marx. New York,
Wiley [1967] 489 p.

Discusses the biological basis of language capacities in the
light of modern advances in technology and methodology in
behavior research. Deals with physiological and neurological
aspects of speech; language acquisition; language in relation
to evolution and genetics; language and cognition. Includes
appendices on 'The formal nature of language', by Noam
Chomsky and 'The history of the biological basis of
language', by Otto Marx. Contains extensive bibliographical
references; illustrations, diagrams; indexes. *Use:* For all
students of language and linguistics, biology, behavioral
sciences, psychology, anthropology and education.

Lyons, John. *Introduction to Theoretical Linguistics.* Cambridge,
126   Cambridge University Press, 1968. 519 p.

Aims to present the most important trends in contemporary
linguistic theory. Deals with the structure of language,

phonetics and phonology, grammar and semantics, focusing on semantics, and on the Chomsky's system of transformational grammar. Includes explanatory notes, bibliography and index. *Use:* Clearly written, it is recommended for all students of linguistics, psychology, anthropology, sociology, computer science, and for general interested readers.

McIntosh, Angus and M. A. K. Halliday. *Patterns of Language: Papers in General, Descriptive and Applied Linguistics.* Bloomington, Indiana University Press [c1966] 199 p. (Indiana University studies in the history and theory of linguistics)   **127**

Contains eleven essays concerned with various aspects of language, some reprinted from journals, the rest previously unpublished, based on the authors' lectures and seminars. *Use:* For students of linguistics, language teachers, scholars in literature, and for interested laymen.

Malmberg, Bertil. *New Trends in Linguistics; an Orientation.* Translated from the Swedish original by Edward Carney. Stockholm [The Nature Method Institutes] 1964. 226 p. (Bibliotheca linguistica: guides to modern theories and methods, vol. 1)   **128**

Attempts to combine scientific accuracy with a popular, nontechnical style in presenting modern European and American linguistics "as practised within different schools and by different individuals". Includes a name index. *Use:* For students and teachers of languages, speech therapists, communication engineers, etc.

Marckwardt, Albert H. *American English.* New York, Oxford University Press, 1958. 194 p.   **129**

Aims to present a synthesis of the growth and development of the English language in America. Focuses on the relationship between language and culture. Discusses differences and similarities with British English, and projects into the future. Index. *Use:* For students in English language and linguistics at all levels, and for general readers.

Martinet, André. *Elements of General Linguistics.* With a foreword by L. R. Palmer. Translated by Elisabeth Palmer. [Chicago] University of Chicago Press [1964] 205 p.   **130**

Important introduction to modern linguistics showing development of this science since de Saussure's *Cours de linguistique generale*. Deals with descriptive and structural linguistics together with its main branches: phonetics, phonemics and morphemics. Presents "the variety of languages and linguistic usage", and "the evolution of languages". Contains brief bibliography and terminological index. *Use:* For all students of linguistics.

131 Martinet, André. *A Functional View of Language*. Oxford, Clarendon Press, 1962. 163 p. (The Waynflete lectures, 1961)

Contains expanded version of five lectures delivered at Oxford in 1961: realism versus formalism; towards a functional syntax; linguistic typology; linguistic variety; linguistic evolution. Focuses attention on dual aspect of language as physical reality and as expression of experience; criticizes the formalists for their static attitude to structure, and gives excellent surveys of the problems of linguistic typology, variety and evolution. Indexes. *Uses:* For students in advanced linguistics courses.

132 Mencken, Henry L. *The American Language; an inquiry into the development of English in the United States*. The 4th ed. and the two supplements, abridged, with annotations and new material by Raven I. MacDavid, Jr. With the assistance of David M. Maurer. [1st abridged ed.] New York, Knopf, 1963. 777 p.

The condensed and updated version of a classic three-volume work, this study covers all aspects of language. The twelve chapters discuss the beginnings and growth of American, comparison of American and British English, the pronunciation, spelling, grammar, proper names and slang of American English, and the future of the English language in general. The editor's changes and annotations are indicated in both the text and the footnotes. Included also is an extensive list of words and phrases. Index. *Use:* For students in English language and linguistics at all levels, and for general readers.

133 Mohrmann, Christine, Alf Sommerfelt and Joshua Whatmough, eds. *Trends in European and American Linguistics, 1930-1960*. Edited on the occasion of the Ninth International Congress of

Linguists, Cambridge, Massachusetts, 27 August–1 September 1962, for the Permanent International Committee of Linguists. Utrecht, Spectrum, 1966. 299 p.

Contains twelve papers on the main trends in general linguistics for the period as stated above. Included are: linguistic prospects in the United States; mathematical linguistics; comparative and historical linguistics in America 1930-1960, linguistics and language teaching in the United States 1940-1960; anthropological linguistics; glossematics; general linguistics–the United States in the fifties; the Bloomfield 'School'; der Stand der Indogermanischen Sprachwissenschaft; orientamenti generali della linguistica in Italia 1930-1960; the French school of linguistics; l'école Saussurienne de Genève.

Ornstein, Jacob and William W. Gage. *The ABC's of Languages and Linguistics.* [1st ed.] Philadelphia, Chilton Books [1964] 205 p. **134**

Aims to give basic information about language and its history. Deals with phonetics, structural analysis, semantics, sociolinguistic problems and world languages. Focuses on "language-handicapped Americans" and discusses a variety of learning programs. *Use:* For students, instructors and interested laymen.

Palmer, F. R., ed. *Selected Papers of J. R. Firth, 1952-1959.* Bloomington, Indiana University Press [1968] 209 p. (Indiana University studies in the history and theory of linguistics) **135**

A selection of twelve papers, seven published previously and five unpublished studies written between the years 1956-57. Included are: "Linguistic analysis as a study of meaning"; "The languages of linguistics"; "Structural linguistics"; "Philology in the Philological Society"; "Linguistic analysis and translation"; "Linguistics and translation"; "Descriptive linguistics and the study of English"; "A new approach to grammar"; "Applications of general linguistics"; "Ethnographic analysis, and language with refernce to Malinowski's views"; "A synopsis of linguistic theory 1930-55"; "The treatment of language in general linguistics". Bibliography of publications by J. R. Firth.

136 Partridge, Eric. *The World of Words; an introduction to language in general and to English and American in particular.* [3rd ed., rev.] London, H. Hamilton [1948] 201 p.

A comprehensive introduction to language and word history. Contains diagrams and indexes. *Use:* For student beginners in English language and linguistics.

137 Partridge, Eric and John W. Clark. *British and American English Since 1900.* With contributions on English in Canada, South Africa, Australia, New Zealand and India. New York, Greenwood Press, 1968 [c1951] 341 p.

Consists of two parts, each discussing the development of British English and American English in the 20th century. Reviews of the book are controversial, but generally agree that the second part, by Professor Clark of University of Minnesota, is very informative and highly readable and should be recommended to all concerned with usage of the contemporary English language. Index.

138 Pike, Kenneth L. *Language in Relation to a Unified Theory of the Structure of Human Behavior.* 2d rev. ed. The Hague, Mouton, 1967. 762 p. (Janua linguarum. Series maior, 24)

Aims to revise the conceptual framework for language study, showing analogies between linguistic structure and the structure of society and of nonverbal behavior. Includes ectensive bibliographical references and index. *Use:* Major scholarly work for linguists, archeologists, sociologists, psychologists, anthropologists and ethnologists.

139 Potter, Simeon. *Modern Linguistics.* New York, W. W. Norton [c1954] 192 p. (The language library. Norton Library, no. 223)

Written in a lucid style, this is a concise introduction to general linguistics, discussing phonology, morphology, syntax, vocabulary, and communication. Included are discussions on some controversial topics in modern linguistics. Contains maps, diagrams, select bibliography and index. *Use:* Meant primarily for general reader. Recommended to student beginners in linguistics.

Quick, Randolph. *The Use of English.* With supplements by A. C. Gimson and Jeremy Warburg. New York, St. Martins Press [1964, c1962] 335 p. **140**

Covers a wide variety of uses of English aiming "to stimulate a mature and informed approach to our language, so that we can understand the nature of English, be encouraged to use it more intelligently, respond to it more sensitively, and acknowledge more fully the implications of its international use today."—Pref. *Use:* Intended for general reader; good source of reference for all concerned with proper use of English.

Robins, Robert H. *General Linguistics; An Introductory Survey.* Bloomington, Indiana University Press [1965, c1964] 390 p. **141**

Survey of general linguistics covering semantics, phonetics, phonology, various aspects of grammar and linguistic studies in relation to other subjects. Stress is put on the British prosodic analysis and on the American descriptive linguistics. Special attention is given to comparative and historical linguistics and the history of linguistics. Most examples are taken from English. Each chapter closes with a bibliography and notes. Index. *Use:* Valuable book, not only for undergraduate students of linguistics for whom it was intended, but also useful to other interested readers.

Sapir, Edward. *Language; An Introduction to the Study of Speech.* New York, Harcourt, Brace & World [1949] 242 p. **142**

First published in 1921. The book discusses many aspects of spoken and written language, its relations to thought, the nature of historical processes, race, culture, art, etc. Technical terms are avoided. Index. Excellent source of reference and a classic in the field of linguistics.

Saussure, Ferdinand de. *Course in General Linguistics.* Ed. by Charles Bally and Albert Sechehaye in collaboration with Albert Riedlinger. Translated from the French by Wade Baskin. New York, McGraw-Hill [c1966] 240 p. **143**

Based on lecture notes collected from the author's students, this book contains the essence of de Saussure's theories which prepared the ground for modern linguistics. The volume consists of several parts dealing with principles of phonology and general principles, and with synchronic, diachronic, geographical and retrospective linguistics. *Use:* Essential to any student of linguistics.

144 Schlauch, Margaret. *The Gift of Language*. New York, Dover [1955] 342 p.

First published as *Gift of Tongues*, in 1942, this is a popular introduction to the science of language, concentrating on comparative and historical linguistics. Supplied with excellent examples, exercises, bibliography and notes and an index. *Use:* For laymen, students and teachers of language and linguistics.

145 Sebeok, Thomas A., ed. *Current Trends in Linguistics*. The Hague, Mouton, 1963-

Contents. -v. 1. Soviet and East European linguistics. -v. 2. Linguistics in East Asia and South East Asia. -v. 3. Theoretical foundations. -v. 4. Ibero-American and Caribbean linguistics. -v. 5. Linguistics in South Asia. Other volumes in the series (most still in preparation) are: -v. 6. Linguistics in South West Asia and North Africa. -v. 7. Linguistics in Sub-Saharan Africa. -v. 8. Linguistics in Oceania. v. 9. Linguistics in Western Europe. -v. 10. Linguistics in North America. -v. 11. Diachronic, areal, and typological linguistics. -v. 12. Linguistics and adjacent arts and sciences. -v. 13. Index to vols. 1-12.

As indicated by titles, volumes in the series cover mainly geopolitical entities, presenting state of significant linguistic activities and research done in areas designated. Besides this organizing principle, several volumes have theoretical instead of areal orientation. E.g. several chapters in volume 3 give consolidated and expanded versions of talks delivered in the Trends in Linguistics Lecture Series at the 1964 Linguistic Institute of the Linguistic Society of America, held at Indiana University. Contributors of the papers included are internationally reknown linguists such as Chomsky, Pike, and Hockett, to name a few. Discussed subjects are of current linguistic interest, for example: language universals, generative grammar, historical linguistics and the genetic relationship, mathematical linguistics, explorations in semantic theory, descriptive and comparative linguistics, and other aspects of linguistic science. Included in each volume are bibliographical references, biographical notes, and indexes.

To Honor Roman Jakobson; Essays on the Occasion of his Seventieth Birthday, 11 October 1966. The Hague, Mouton, **146** 1967. 3 vols. (Janua linguarum. Series maior, 31-33)

International in scope, timeless in coverage, this is a collection of essays by well-known contemporary linguists and literary historians, discussing many aspects of language and linguistics. Texts in English, French, German, Italian, Latin, Russian, Serbo-Croatian and Spanish. Includes a bibliography of the publications of Roman Jakobson.

Uitti, Karl D. *Linguistics and Literary Theory.* Englewood Cliffs, N. J., Prentice-Hall [1969] 272 p. (The Princeton studies: **147** humanistic scholarship in America)

Discusses contemporary American research on both linguistics and literary theory. Shows that the present separate status of these two independent branches of learning has not always been the case in past cultural and philosophical traditions. Analyses main characteristics of the Western concept of language, deals with linguistics and literary study as practiced in the United States and abroad recently, and gives suggestions regarding interrelations between two field. Contains index. *Use:* A book "directed to informed and interested readers" (Pref.), it is recommended to students of linguistics and philosophy of language at all levels.

Vachek, Josef. *The Linguistic School of Prague; An Introduction to its Theory and Practice.* Bloomington, Indiana University **148** Press, 1966. 184 p.

Presents a revised series of lectures given by the author at the Linguistic Institute, Indiana University, in 1964. Gives historical background of the Prague Linguistic Circle (founded in 1926), and discusses its theories of language, problems of phonology, morphology, syntax, etc. Includes appendixes containing biographical notes on forty-six members of the Circle; bibliographies; indexes. Complements the author's *Prague School Reader in Linguistics* (1964).

149 Vachek, Josef, comp. *A Prague School Reader in Linguistics.* Bloomington, Indiana University Press [1966, c1964] 485 p.

Contains forty important papers written by the members of the Prague Linguistic Circle between the years of 1928 and 1948. Includes works by Mathesius, Trnka, Trubetzkoy, Jakobson and Vachek. Presented in their original languages the papers are in English, French and German; those originally in Czech or Russian are given in English translation. No index.

150 Whorf, Benjamin L. *Language: Thought and Reality; Selected Writings.* Ed. and with an introd. by John B. Carroll. Foreword by Stuart Chase. Cambridge, Mass., M.I.T. Press [1956] 278 p.

Collection of papers dealing with various aspects of language and linguistics. Stress is put on the hypothesis that the structure of one's language influences thinking and understanding of one's environment. *Use:* Essential to all students of linguistics. *See also* 165, 179, 241.

HISTORY OF LINGUISTICS

151 Dinneen, Francis P. *An Introduction to General Linguistics.* New York, Holt, Rinehart and Winston [c1967] 452 p.

Book based on lectures given to students in the Institute of Languages and Linguistics of Georgetown University. It deals with the development of general linguistics from ancient to present times. Much of the material is devoted to the nineteenth century and also to the contributions made by modern scholars, especially: de Saussure, Sapir, Bloomfield, Firth, Hjelmslev and Chomsky. Included in the book is a glossary of the linguistic terms. Excellent bibliographies. Index. *Use:* For linguists and literary historians.

152 Dixon, Robert. M. W. *What Is Language? A New Approach to Linguistic Description.* [London] Longmans [c1965] 216 p. [Longmans linguistics Library]

Aims to present a new scheme for linguistic description whereby each component of the scheme is given theoretical description and illustrated by examples from spontaneous English conversation. Discusses correlations between language patterns and other behavioral or situational patterns, as well as correlations wholly inside language. Includes a survey of philosophical and linguistic opinions about language, from Plato and Aristotle to Wittgenstein, Chomsky and Halliday. Bibliography. Index. *Use:* For all students of linguistics, logic, psychology and philosophy, concerned with the history and theory of language.

Ivić, Milka. *Trends in Linguistics.* Translated by Muriel Heppell. The Hague, Mouton, 1965. 260 p. (Janua linguarum. Series minor, nr. 42)　　**153**

An important concise history of linguistics, focusing on theories of the most prominent contemporary linguists. Discusses basic characteristics and trends of development of the twentieth century scholarship, non-structural and structural linguistics, logical symbolism in linguistics, linguistic syntax and the generative approach, and mathematical linguistics. Includes excellent bibliographical references and indexes. *Use:* Recommended to all teachers and students of linguistics, particularly to those concerned with the history of language and linguistics.

Leroy, Maurice. *The Main Trends in Modern Linguistics.* Translated [from the French] by Glanville Price. Oxford, Blackwell, 1967. 155 p.　　**154**

A historical survey of linguistics from ancient to modern times. Stresses development of the science of language in the nineteenth and the twentieth centuries. Attaches special significance to the works of the European scholars, particularly de Saussure. Indexes. *Use:* Book meant as "a fundamental part of a young linguist's training. [Its] aim has not been to produce a work of erudition [and so] references have been kept to a minimum. However, such brief indications as are given well enable the reader to compile a bibliography for any aspect he wishes to study further".—Pref.

155 Pedersen, Holger. *The Discovery of Language; Linguistic Science in the Nineteenth Century.* Translated by John Webster Spargo. Bloomington, Indiana University Press [1962, c1959] 360 p.

First published as *Linguistic Science in the Nineteenth Century*, in 1931, this is an important, detailed history of linguistic studies, focusing on the development of Indo-European comparative linguistics. Includes portraits, maps, and indexes. *Use:* For all concerned with the history of linguistics.

156 Robins, R. H. *A Short History of Linguistics.* Bloomington, Indiana University Press [1968, c1967] 248 p.

An account of the history of linguistic studies from ancient times to the present day. Contains a brief bibliography and an index. *Use:* Essential to both teachers and students of linguistics.

157 Sebeok, Thomas A., ed. *Portraits of Linguists; A Biographical Source Book for the History of Western Linguistics, 1746-1963.* Bloomington, Indiana University Press, 1966. 2 vols.

Text in English, French and German. Valuable source of information, although very selective. Arranged chronologically by the subjects' year of birth, it includes ninety biographical sketches of prominent linguists and philologists. Index.

158 Waterman, John T. *Perspectives in Linguistics.* Chicago, University of Chicago Press [1963] 105 p.

A short historical survey of linguistics from ancient to modern times. Stresses importance of works of the nineteenth and the twentieth century scholars to recent development of structural linguistics as a science. Includes: table of phonetic symbols, selected bibliography, and index. *Use:* Excellent source of information to anyone interested in the history of language. *See also* 91, 106, 108, 115, 118, 141.

GRAMMARS

General

Curme, George D. *English Grammar.* New York, Barnes & Noble [c1947] 308 p. (College outline series, 61) **159**

First published in 1925, and meant as a textbook for college courses, this is a concise, practical guide to English grammar and usage. Includes many examples from literary works showing development of the language through centuries. Supplied with index and cross-references. *Use:* A good source of reference to students, teachers and general users.

Francis, Winthrop N. *The Structure of American English.* With chapter on American English dialects by Raven I. McDavid, Jr., **160** New York, Ronald Press [1958] 614 p.

A survey of English grammar based on modern descriptive linguistics. Discusses: language and linguistics, phonetics, phonemics, morphemics, grammar (parts of speech, syntactic structures, sentences), graphics, the dialects of American English, and linguistics and the teacher of English. Includes appendix, glossary, bibliography and index. *Use:* For upper-division undergraduates, and for graduate students new to the science of language.

Hill, Archibald A. *Introduction to Linguistic Structures; From Sound to Sentence in English.* New York, Harcourt, Brace & **161** World [c1958] 496 p.

While not intended as a complete reference grammar, this book presents a well balanced view of English structure, from the smallest elements, sounds, through morphology, up to complete elements, sentences. Includes appendixes and index. *Use:* For undergraduates and graduate students in English language and linguistics.

Jespersen, Otto. *Essentials of English Grammar.* University, Ala., University of Alabama Press [1964] 387 p. (Alabama linguistic **162** and philological series, 1)

A reprint of the 1933 edition, based on *Philosophy of Grammar* and *Modern English Grammar*, this is an excellent, comprehensive and standard work, emphasising the sound system of the language and using traditional terminology. Index. *Use:* For teachers and students of grammar at all levels, and for general users.

163 Jespersen, Otto. *A Modern English Grammar on Historical Principles.* London, Allen & Unwin [1940-1961] 7 vols.

Contents. -Pt. 1. Sounds and spellings. 4th ed. -Pt. 2. Syntax. First volume. 3d ed. -Pt. 3. Syntax. Second volume. -Pt. 4. Syntax. Third volume. -Pt. 5. Syntax. Fourth volume. -Pt. 6. Morphology. -Pt. 7. Syntax, completed and ed. by Niels Haislund.

A classic in the field, it continues to be an excellent source of reference on English grammar. Contains numerous examples from English literature. Indexes. *Use:* To all concerned with English grammar and the history of language.

164 Joos, Martin. *The English Verb; form and meanings.* Madison, University of Wisconsin Press, 1964. 251 p.

Important and interesting work on the English verb systems, it is based on the study of Sybille Bedford's book, *The Trial of Dr. Adams* (data provided by the courtroom notes from the famous murder case). Linguistic analysis employed here to examine a variety of verb phrases is based on a number of categories of English usage: infinitive and presentative modals, assertion, tense, aspect and phrase, voice and function. Contains appendix and index. *Use:* For linguists, students and teachers of English language and linguistics at all levels.

165 Lamb, Sydney M. *Outline of Stratificational Grammar.* With an appendix by Leonard E. Newell. Washington, D. C., Georgetown University Press [c1966] 109 p.

A revised and expanded version of the author's 1962 *Outline*, providing for changes in terminology, notation, and discoveries of new properties of linguistic structure made since 1962. There are three parts: introduction; linguistic structure; and linguistic description; each with further subdivisions. Contains bibliography, exercises, diagrams, appendix, index. *Use:* For students in advanced linguistics courses.

Palmer, Frank R. *A Linguistic Study of the English Verb.* [London] Longmans [c1965] 199 p. (Longmans' linguistics library) **166**

Analyses verbs of modern English language in various grammatical categories. Deals with the auxiliary verbs; the full verbs; the simple phrase; BE, HAVE and DO; the complex phrase, and phrasal verbs and prepositional verbs. Includes verb and subject indexes.

Roberts, Paul. *Patterns of English.* New York, Harcourt, Brace & World [c1956] 314 p. **167**

Written in a simple, lucid style, this basic English grammar is meant for students and instructors alike. Divided into ten parts, and sixty-four chapters, each followed by exercises, it deals with form classes, structure groups, basic patterns and function units, pattern parts and the underlying sound. Index.

Sledd, James H. *A Short Introduction to English Grammar.* Chicago, Scott, Foresman [1959] 346 p. **168**

Aims to combine the conventional approaches to language description with the principles and methods of contemporary linguistics. Discusses: the sounds of English, parts of speech, nominal sequences, verbal sequences, subjects and predicates, and the sentence and its kinds. Contains a glossary of grammatical terms. Concludes with a section on applied grammar and notes on English prose style. Includes numerous exercises, bibliographies, index, and correction chart. *Use:* Addressed especially to undergraduate and graduate students of American colleges, particularly to those in English departments; to prospective teachers of English, to students and instructors in language history, composition, and in beginning courses in linguistics.

Strang, Barbara M. H. *Modern English Structure.* 2d ed. New York, St. Martin's Press, 1968. 264 p. **169**

Presents a descriptive analysis of current English, supported with quotations from the writings of British and American linguists. Emphasises spoken language, but uses traditional terminology. Gives many examples from literary sources. Includes diagrams, spectrograms, bibliography and index. Most chapters are supplied with suggestions for exercises and further reading. *Use:* Meant primarily as an introductory textbook for students at elementary level, it ought to be also very useful to teachers of English language and linguistics.

170   Whitehall, Harold. *Structural Essentials of English.* New York, Harcourt, Brace & World [c1956] 154 p.

An introduction to linguistics, aiming to describe the general structural design of English and to focus on particular difficulties encountered in the process of leaning to write the language. *Use:* For teachers of English and students of composition. *See also* 10, 31, 99, 176, 194.

Generative–Transformational

171   Bach, Emmon. *An Introduction to Transformational Grammars.* New York, Holt, Rinehart and Winston [1964] 205 p.

A comprehensive presentation of transformational grammatical theory developed since the publication of Chomsky's *Syntactic Structures* in 1957. Discusses the task and data of linguistics, some basic notions, phrase-structure rules, grammatical transformations, problems of syntactic analysis, the phonological component, the form of grammars, and problems and prospects. Includes a selected bibliography, index, and index of special symbols. *Use:* For students acquainted with modern descriptive linguistics.

172   Chomsky, Noam. *Cartesian Linguistics: A Chapter in the History of Rationalist Thought.* [1st ed.] New York, Harper & Row [1966] 119 p. (Studies in language)

An essay on importance of rationalist theories of language from Descartes, through the eighteenth and nineteenth centuries, to the present day studies of grammatical structure. Deals with: creative aspect of language use; deep and surface structure, description and explanation in linguistics; acquisition and use of language. Includes extensive notes and a bibliography. *Use:* For students of linguistics and general readers alike.

Chomsky, Noam. *Syntactic Structures.* The Hague, Mouton, 1965. 118 p. (Janua linguarum series, 4) **173**

First published in 1957, this is the notable presentation of the author's theory of linguistic structure. Emphasis is put on a transformational-generative model, considered by Chomsky the best of the three models for grammatical analysis. Contains two appendixes and a bibliography. *Use:* Essential to all students of linguistics.

Chomsky, Noam. *Topics in the Theory of Generative Grammar.* The Hague, Mouton, 1966. 95 p. (Janua linguarum, Series **174**
minor, nr. 56)

Contains texts of four lectures delivered at the Linguistic Institute of the Linguistic Society of America, held at Indiana University, June, 1964: assumptions and goals; discussion of criticisms; the theory of transformational generative grammar; some problems in phonology. Includes a bibliography.

Jacobs, Roderick A. and Peter S. Rosenbaum. *English Transformational Grammar.* With an epilogue by Paul M. Postal. **175**
Waltham, Mass., Blaisdell [c1968] 294 p. (A Blaisdell book in the humanities)

Deals with deep and surface structures and transformational rules in languages, in general, and with deep structure and transformations in the English language in particular. There are twenty-nine chapters put into six selections: the study of language; constituents and features, segment transformations and syntactic processes; sentence embedding; simplicity and linguistic explanation; and conjunction. Includes an epilogue, summaries and exercises after each chapter, and index. *Use:* Intended for use in courses at both undergraduate and graduate school level.

Katz, Jerrold J. and Paul M. Postal. *An Integrated Theory of Linguistic Descriptions.* Cambridge, Mass., MIT Press [c1964] **176**
178 p. (MIT Press research monograph series, no. 26)

Deals with a theory of the nature of language and aims "to provide an adequate means of incorporating the grammatical and the semantic descriptions of a language into one integrated description. The conception of all linguistic description proposed here combines the generative conception of grammar developed by Chomsky with the conception of semantics proposed by Katz and Fodor".–Pref. Includes bibliography.

177 Koutsoudas, Andreas. *Writing Transformational Grammars: an introduction.* New York, McGraw-Hill [1966] 368 p.

Meant primarily as a text for an introductory course in syntax, this book aims to help the reader learn the theory and practice of generative transformational grammar, originated by Noam Chomsky. Discussed in the first three chapters are theoretical backgrounds and morphophonemics. The last five chapters focus on a particular syntactic notion; i.e. co-occurrence relations, agreement, permutation, conjoining, and embedding. Included in each chapter are problems, solutions, notes and a set of exercises graded according to difficulty. *Use:* For student beginners in transformational grammar.

178 Lees, Robert B. *The Grammar of English Nominalizations.* Bloomington, Ind., Indiana University, 1966 [c1963] (Indiana, University Research Center in Anthropology, Folklore and Linguistics)

Revised version of a doctoral dissertation, this monograph analyses various nominal expressions, applying the rules of transformational grammar. Supplied with three appendixes: A. English nominal phrases. B. Comparison with German nominals. C. Brief sketch of Turkish nominals. Bibliography. *Use:* This specialized study is recommended to linguists, upper level undergraduates and graduate students in linguistics only.

179 Reibel, David A. and Sanford A. Schane, eds. *Modern Studies in English; readings in transformational grammar.* Englewood-Cliffs, N. J., Prentice-Hall [1969] 481 p.

An anthology of articles on the transformational syntax of English written over the past decade. Divided into six sections, the papers deal with fundamental questions in linguistics from the transformational point of view (pt. 1, 'Background'); treat specific aspects of English structure (pts. 2-5, 'Conjunction', 'Pronominalization', 'Realitivization');

and discuss application of the insights of transformational grammar to historical change, language acquisition, metrics, and language teaching (pt. 6, 'Applications and implications'). Contributors include: Chomsky, Halle, Lees, Langacker, Fillmore, and others. Includes bibliographical footnotes. *Use:* For all concerned with modern linguistic theories, transformational grammar, and language teaching.

Rosenbaum, Peter S. *The Grammar of English Predicate Complement Constructions.* Cambridge, Mass., M.I.T. Press [1967] **180**
128 p. (M.I.T. research monograph series, 47)

An introduction to the study of abstract syntax and to the general problems of complex sentence formation, focusing on noun and verb phrases, and closing with a study of a historical perspective (i.e. the work of Chomsky and others in the field of generative transformational grammar). Includes appendix listing verb classifications, and index. *Use:* For linguists and students in upper level linguistic courses.

Thomas, Owen. *Transformational Grammar and the Teacher of English.* New York, Holt, Rinehart and Winston [1965] 240 p. **181**

Meant primarily for teachers of English, this is a "pedagogical rather than scientific grammar." (Pref.) Deals with the function and nature of grammar, basic English word and sentence structures, and focuses on grammar and the school. Contains very useful summaries and topics for discussions after each chapter, a short annotated bibliography, and index. *Use:* Very good introduction to transformational grammar for all concerned. *See also* 13, 85, 191, 225, 227, 282.

Tagmemic

Cook, Walter A. *Introduction to Tagmemic Analysis.* New York, Holt, Rinehart and Winston [1969] 210 p. (Transatlantic series **182**
in linguistics)

An application of the methods of linguistic science to practical language problems, dealing with inductive process for analyzing languages. The author explains the tagmemic system and presents grammatical structures at the sentence, clause, phrase and word levels. The work is based on the writings of Pike, Longacre, Elson, Pickett and other tagmemic authors. Includes supplementary exercises, tagmemic symbols, selected bibliography and index. *Use:* For students beginning language analysis and for those who are analyzing an unknown language for the first time.

183 Cook, Walter A. *On Tagmemes and Transforms.* Washington, D. C., Georgetown University Press [1967] 67 p.

An exposition of tagmemic analysis, a unique form of grammatical system, developed by the Summer Institute of Linguistics and based mainly on the recent works of Pike, Chomsky, Elson and Longacre. Consists of three parts: Pt. 1, "On tagmemes"; Pt. 2, "On transforms"; Pt. 3, "The tagmemic-transformational model". Includes a bibliography and a list of tagmemic symbols. *Use:* This specialized work is recommended to grammarians and advanced students of linguistics concerned with new developments in the science of language.

184 Longacre, Robert E. *Grammar Discovery Procedures; a field manual.* The Hague, Mouton, 1964. 162 p. (Janua linguarum. Series minor, nr. 33)

Meant as an aid to grammatical description of little known languages, it is also an exposition of the theory of grammar-tagmemics, discussing the suggested procedures on clause, phrase, word and sentence levels. Includes tables, diagrams, bibliography and index. *Use:* This important work deals with the nature and structure of language in the light of the tagmemic tradition of the school of American linguists founded by Pike. The book is recommended to all linguists and grammarians.

Systemic

185 Halliday, Michael A. K. *Intonation and Grammar in British English.* The Hague, Mouton, 1967. 61 p. (Janua linguarum. Series practica, 48)

A revised reprint of two previously published papers, "The tones of English" and "Intonation in English Grammar", this book is based on a study of recorded texts featuring "informal educated spoken Southern British", but acceptable as "standard British". Discusses intonation patterns in their relationship to grammar and the language as a whole in terms of his theory of "systemic" grammar. Includes tables, diagrams and bibliography. *Use:* For teachers and students of language and linguistics. *See also* 282.

HISTORY OF LANGUAGE AND HISTORICAL LINGUISTICS

Baugh, Albert C. *A History of the English Language.* 2d ed. New York, Appleton-Century-Crofts [c1957] 506 p.   **186**

A revised edition of a well-known and old (1935) textbook for college students, aiming "to preserve a proper balance between what may be called internal history—sounds and inflections—and external history—the political, social and intellectual forces that have determined the course of that development at different periods."—Pref. Discusses the present state and the future of English; surveys the history of language from its Indo-European origins, through centuries, up to the modern times; dwells on foreign influences, and on a variety of dialects; devotes a chapter to the English language in America. Includes maps, extensive bibliographies and index. Two appendixes contain specimens of the Middle English dialects, and English spelling. *Use:* For all interested in the history of the English language.

Bloomfield, Leonard. *Language History; from Language (1933 ed.).* Edited by Harry Hoijer. New York, Holt, Rinehart and Winston [c1965] 281-512 p.   **187**

"*Language history* is a reprint of chapters 17-27 of Leonard Bloomfield's *Language* (1933) made from the original plates without any editorial revision or renumbering of pages.

Bloomfield's notes to each chapter and his extensive bibliography have been replaced by a new set of Notes and a Bibliography prepared by the editor, primarily for the purpose of explaining the many cross-references in Chapters 17-27 to chapters not reprinted and to supply the reader with references to material published since 1933."—Pref.

188 Bloomfield, Morton W. & Leonard Newmark. *A Linguistic Introduction to the History of English.* New York, Knopf, 1965 [c1963] 375 p.

Applies modern linguistic principles to the history of English, intending "to expose the student to ways of looking at the language" rather than present him with the results of previous studies. Uses viewpoints of different schools of linguistics in dealing with various stages of historical development. Consists of eight chapters discussing: language and the history of language; phonology and modern English; comparative linguistics and the Indo-European family of languages; the morphology of Old English; the dialects of Middle English; grammar and early modern English; the problem of correctness and good usage: 1600-1850; the English vocabulary and English word formation. Contains a selective bibliography of works of general and historical linguistics published before 1962; index of morphemes, words and phrases; and a general index. *Use:* For all students and teachers concerned with the history of the English language and linguistics.

189 Bryant, Margaret M. *Modern English and Its Heritage.* 2d ed. New York, Macmillan [c1962] 492 p.

A college textbook discussing the history of the language, speech sounds and letters, words, and grammar and usage. Contains bibliographies, lists of topics for class discussions and research papers, and index. *Use:* For students of English language and linguistics at all levels, and for interested laymen.

190 Hoenigswald, Henry M. *Language Change and Linguistic Reconstruction.* Chicago, University of Chicago Press [1960] 168 p.

Aims to develop a procedure for analyzing linguistic changes in the history of a language, based on the semantic, grammatical, and phonemic systems. Includes bibliography and index. *Use:* Difficult to read, this book is recommended for students advanced in linguistics.

King, Robert D. *Historical Linguistics and Generative Grammar.* Englewood Cliffs, N. J. Prentice-Hall [1969] 230 p. **191**

The book aims to be comprehensive in presenting historical linguistics as it is now understood by linguists following Chomsky and Halle. Discusses competence and performance together with general grammatical components (semantic, transformational and phonological). Deals with primary change, grammar simplification, sound change and analogy, syntax, reconstruction, causality of change, and scribal practice. Includes supplementary reading lists, bibliography and index. *Use:* For students of linguistics beyond introductory level.

Lehmann, Winifred P. *Historical Linguistics: An Introduction.* New York, Holt, Rinehart and Winston [c1962] 297 p. **192**

Introductory textbook stressing Indo-European languages, mainly English. Covers: the classification of languages; methods employed in the gathering and analysis of material; change in language (in its phonological, grammatical and other aspects). Contains annotated bibliography and index. *Use:* For students and instructors concerned with methods used in historical linguistics.

Lehmann, Winifred P. and Yakov Malkiel, eds. *Directions for Historical Linguistics; A Symposium.* Austin, University of **193** Texas [1968] 199 p.

Important publication based on the 1966 University of Texas symposium, aiming "to restore historical studies to their position of leadership among the primary linguistic disciplines." (Pref.) Focuses on changes in grammar rather than phonology. Includes five papers: "Saussure's dichotomy between descriptive and historical linguistics", by W. P. Lehmann; "The inflectional paradigm as an occasional determinant of sound change", by Y. Malkiel, "The notion of morpho(pho)neme", J. Kurylowicz; "Mutations of linguistic categories", by E. Benveniste; and "Empirical foundations for a theory of language change", by U. Weinreich, W. Labov and M. Herzog. Includes bibliography and index. *Use:* For those concerned with historical linguistics, grammar, and sociolinguistics. The last section of the book recommended to all students of language and linguistics.

194 Nist, John. *A Structural History of English.* New York, St. Martin's Press [1966] 426 p.

Combines a traditional history-of-the-language approach with modern linguistic analysis. Describes phonology, morphology, syntax, and formal stylistics at each stage of historical development. Deals with the present status and structure of the language; discusses historical and structural factors that shaped today's English; focuses on American English; and assesses the future of the language in usage, influence, and academic study. Includes questions for research and discussion and selective bibliography after each chapter; a selective glossary, and index. *Use:* Intended for a one-semester or a two-semester course in the English language; recommended to all students in language and linguistics. *See also* 17, 108, 115, 141, 144, 163.

PHONETICS

195 Abercrombie, David. *Elements of General Phonetics.* Chicago, Aldine [1967] 203 p.

Written in a clear simple language, the book is addressed to a reader with no previous knowledge of phonetics and can be used as a primary source of information on phonetics for any language. Includes bibliographies and subject index.

Bronstein, Arthur J. *The Pronunciation of American English; an introduction to phonetics.* New York, Appleton-Century-Crofts [1960] 320 p. **196**

Analyses the sounds of American English. Presents the study in three main parts, dealing with: our language today (basic concepts, definitions, attitudes); the sounds of American English (consonants, vowels, formation and acoustic values of sounds, their modification and regional variations); sounds and context (special aspects of the sound system: the nature and types of sound changes, pronunciation of words, pitch levels, stress, and pause). Includes bibliographical references, illustrations, diagrams, tables, maps; exercises and questions for review after each chapter. *Use:* Intended primarily for American university students in phonetics classes, recommended to all concerned with public speaking, dramatics, diction, radio and television performance, and any other areas of study where correct pronunciation of English is essential.

Crystal, David. *Prosodic Systems and Intonation in English.* Cambridge, University Press, 1969. 381 p. (Cambridge studies in linguistics, 1) **197**

The author tries to develop a theoretical basis for the study of intonation in English, by emphasizing the need for intonational phenomena to be integrated within a more general theory of non-segmental phonology. Discusses procedural difficulties and reviews the history of work on the subject. Outlines various concepts required for the study of sound and relates them to the linguistic notions of voice-quality and prosodic system. Covers in separate chapters the prosodic features and intonation system of English, also the grammar and the semantics of intonation. Extensive bibliography and indexes included. *Use:* For phoneticians, grammarians and for specialized linguistic research.

Heffner, Roe-Merrill S. *General Phonetics.* With a foreword by W. F. Twaddell. Madison, University of Wisconsin Press, 1964 [c1950] 253 p. **198**

Deals with physiology and physics of speech sounds. Given also is a brief description of the hearing mechanism. The transcription (IPA alphabet) is used for recording of the phonetic details of language. Supplied with illustrations, charts and diagrams. Includes bibliographic notes and commentary; index. *Use:* For all interested in general problems of phonetics.

199 Jakobson, Roman and Morris Halle. *Fundamentals of Language.* 's-Gravenhage, Mouton, 1956. 87 p. (Janua linguarum, nr. 1)

Important contribution to modern linguistic theory, it deals, in part I, with phonology and phonetics, and presents, in part II, two aspects of language and two types of aphasic disturbances. Includes a supplement—"selected list of studies in general phonology (1931-1955)".

200 Jakobson, Roman, C. Gunnar, M. Fant and Morris Halle. *Preliminaries to Speech Analysis: the distinctive features and their correlates.* [2d print. with additions and corrections] Cambridge [Acoustics Laboratory] Massachusetts Institute of Technology [1963] 64 p. (Massachusetts Institute of Technology. Acoustics Laboratory. Technical reports, 13)

First published in 1952. Written in a technical style, this is an important contribution to phonetic theory focusing on distinctive features of sound units of language and stressing the value of scientific laboratory (acoustic) experiments. Includes diagrams, bibliographical references and indexes. *Use:* For linguists, psychologists, physiologists and neurologists dealing with speech, hearing and language disturbances, communication and electronics engineers, and for students in symbolic logic and semiotics.

201 Jones, Daniel. *The Phoneme: Its Nature and Use.* 2nd ed. Cambridge [Eng.] W. Heffer [1962] 267 p.

An important source of information on various aspects of phonetics, particularly phoneme and its historical development, with examples from seventy-four languages and dialects. Contains list of phonetic symbols and diacritical marks. Included are several indexes and bibliographies.

Kingdon, Roger. *English Intonation Practice.* With conversational texts by N. C. Scott. [London] Longmans [1958] 184 p.　　**202**

Aims to help foreigners speak the language with correct stressing and intonation (British). Includes chapters on stresses and tones, simple tunes, compound and complex tunes, and Shakespearean extracts. Provides graded exercises using texts of conversations, drama, anecdotes, prose and verse. Includes a table of the tonetic stress-marks.

Kingdon, Roger. *The Groundwork of English Stress.* [London] Longmans [1966, c1958] 224 p.　　**203**

Meant primarily to assist foreign students in the proper use of English word stress, this is a helpful companion book to *The Groundwork of English Intonation.* Deals with interdependence of stress and tone, various kinds, degrees and changes of stress, word stress tendencies in English, compound words of different origins with emphasis on English-type compounds and components, and British and American stress differences. Includes a glossary of technical terms and special usages.

Ladefoged, Peter. *Elements of Acoustic Phonetics.* [Chicago] University of Chicago Press [1962] 118 p.　　**204**

Presents basic aspects of acoustics. Focuses on: sound waves, loudness and pitch, quality, wave analysis, resonance, hearing, and the production of speech. Includes a glossary, a brief annotated bibliography and an index. *Use:* For linguists and phoneticians.

Malmberg, Bertil. *Phonetics.* New York, Dover [1963] 123 p.　　**205**

Based on the third edition of the author's *La Phonetique,* published in France in 1954, this is a good concise introduction to the study of sounds of language. Deals with acoustic, physiological, combinatory, experimental, functional (phonemics), and evolutionary phonetics. Discusses types of articulation, vowels, consonants, classification of the sounds in language, quantity, accents, and importance and practical applications of phonetics. Includes table of the

International Phonetic Alphabet, bibliography, diagrams, and index. *Use:* For student beginners in phonetics.

Pike, Kenneth L. *Phonetics; a critical analysis of phonetic theory*
206   *and a technic for the practical description of sounds.* Ann Arbor, University of Michigan Press [1961, c1943] 182 p. (University of Michigan Publications. Language and literature, 21)

Provides basic analysis of the formation of sounds. Gives definitions of sound units and discusses their practical application. Contains bibliography and index. *Use:* For students of general phonetics.

Potter, Ralph K., George A. Kopp, and Harriet Green Kopp.
207   *Visible Speech.* New York, Dover Publications [1966] 439 p.

First published in 1947. Discusses in non-technical language the recording of an analysis of speech by means of the sound spectograph and direct translation methods. This book is a landmark in acoustic phonetics in that it discloses a foundation for work on speaker identification, automatic recognition of speech, the improvement of electrical speech communication facilities and voice coding devices, and the construction of speaking machines. Included are numerous illustrations and diagrams; two appendixes: "Reference listing of phonetic symbols, key words and Webster's diacritical markings", and "Summary of the profiles and hub areas of the non-vowel sounds in a male and female voice"; bibliography of technical publications on visible speech; index. *Use:* Important for all students in university phonetics courses; research workers in language and acoustics laboratories; teachers of deaf; and for all concerned with teaching and learning of physiology, physics and psychology of speech.

Schubiger, Maria. *English Intonation, Its Form and Function.*
208   Tübingen, M. Niemeyer, 1958. 112 p.

Presents material in two main parts, graded according to the text difficulties. First part, "Intonation proper", deals with the tone-patterns of English, and the function of intonation proper. Second part, "Intonation conditioned by sentence-stress", discusses variations conditioned by the context, variations conditioned by sentence structure, and variations engendered by emotion. Includes a bibliography. *Use:* "For students of English desirous of acquiring a correct intonation" (Foreword), and for linguists as an aid to practical intonation exercises.

Stetson, Raymond H. *Motor Phonetics, A Study of Speech Movements in Action.* 2d ed. Amsterdam, Published for Oberlin College by North-Holland Pub. Co., 1951. 212 p. **209**

Discusses application of the analysis of skilled movements to the processes of speech. Uses a syllable, "the simplest possible utterance" (vowels and consonants in acoustic and linguistic analysis) as the unit of experimentation. Employs differences in stress and rate of utterance of a series of syllables as the method of study in most phases of motor phonetics. Includes diagrams, bibliography, glossary of motor phonetic terms and indexes. *Use:* For linguists and students of phonetics beyond introductory level.

Thomas, Charles K. *An Introduction to the Phonetics of American English.* 2d ed. New York, Ronald Press [1958] 273 p. **210**

Designed primarily for elementary courses in phonetics or voice and speech improvement, this book presents a series of graded units, each meant as an assignment or a group of assignments. Analyses the mechanism of speech and classification of speech sounds, the variety of sounds of English, stress, and phonetic changes. Discusses regional variants in American pronunciation, regional transcriptions, and standards of pronunciation. Includes bibliography and index.

Wijk, Axel. *Rules of Pronunciation for the English Language; an account of the relationship between English spelling and pronunciation.* London, Oxford University Press, 1966. 159 p. (Language and language learning, 12) **211**

First published in Sweden in 1965 (?) Discusses both British and American English, focusing on British spelling and pronunciation and pointing out American deviations. Uses two phonetic transcriptions. Includes sections on stressed vowels and diphthongs, the consonants, stress, quantity, and spelling reform proposals. *Use:* For students of English language and linguistics. *See also* 108, 185, 214, 283.

PHONOLOGY

212 Chomsky, Noam and Morris Halle. *The Sound Pattern of English.* New York, Harper and Row [c1968] 470 p. (Studies in language)

> A study of sound structure and a detailed analysis of English phonological theory, presented on the background of historical development. Stresses the rules governing the modern English phonology. Includes bibliography and several indexes. *Use:* For instructors and students beyond introductory courses.

213 Harms, Robert T. *Introduction to Phonological Theory.* Englewood Cliffs, N. J., Prentice-Hall [1968] 142 p.

> Discusses basic problems in generative phonology. Expects the reader to have some knowledge of articulatory phonetics, the phonemic principle (works by Sapir, Jakobson, Halle), and the transformational grammar (works by Bach, Chomsky). Includes chapters on: "The choice of a universal phonetic system"; "Systematic phonemics and systematic phonetics"; "The classification features"; "Phonological rules"; "Rule components"; "Junctures, syllables and morpheme features". Accompanied by exercises; bibliography; indexes. *Use:* Intended for undergraduate courses in phonology, following phonetics and a general introduction to linguistics.

214 Jakobson, Roman. *Selected Writings.* Vol. 1, *Phonological Studies.* 's-Gravenhage, Mouton, 1962. 678 p.

> This volume includes most of the phonological studies written by Jakobson alone or jointly with E. Colin Cherry, Morris Halle and John Lotz, from 1916 to 1961. Contains reprints of thirty-eight papers in English, French, German and Russian, concerned with phonology and phonetics, phonemic theory, phonology of prosody, principles of diachronic and descriptive phonology, speech development of children and language pathology. Physiological, physical, psychological and linguistic aspects of language description are presented in acoustic and articulatory terms. Distinctive ("correlational") feature analysis is applied as linguistic

criterion to phonemic descriptions of specific languages. The final chapter, "Retrospect", is the author's inquiry into the relations between sound and meaning. Indexes. *Use:* For linguists, speech scientists, physiologists, psychologists, and teachers of modern languages.

Lieberman, Philip. *Intonation, Perception, and Language.* Cambridge, Mass., M.I.T. Press [1967] 210 p. (M.I.T. research **215** monograph 38)

Presents a detailed linguistic analysis of some aspects of the intonation of American English and the problem of intonation for all tongues, based on acoustic, perceptual, phonetic, and syntactic data for related and unrelated languages. Focuses on two features underlying the intonation of American English, the 'breath-group' and 'prominence'. Includes bibliographical references and index. *Use:* Written in a technical style, this study is intended for linguists and experimental workers in speech analysis and synthesis.

Pike, Kenneth L. *Phonemics; A Technique for Reducing Languages to Writing.* Ann Arbor, University of Michigan Press, **216** 1947. 254 p.

A classic textbook in phonology, intended to assist students in analyzing the structure of the sound systems of a language. Consists of two parts: pt. 1, analysis and production of phonetic units; pt. 2, analysis and description of phonemic units. Appendix contains remarks on how to learn a language, the international phonetic alphabet, and glossary and index. Included are tables, diagrams, illustrations and problems for solution.

Postal, Paul M. *Aspects of Phonological Theory.* New York, Harper & Row [1968] 326 p. **217**

This book discusses "the relative merits of autonomous and systematic phonemics".—Pref. It is concerned with criticism of autonomous phonology, independent of grammatical structure, and with presentation of a more adequate theory acceptable to generative linguistic description. Deals, in part 1, with a variety of synchronic matters founded on the relative adequacy of the autonomous and systematic conceptions, and focuses, in part 2, on the diachronic phonology and the nature of the "sound change". Much of the book's material is based on the study of the Northern Iroquoian languages, mostly Mohawk. Bibliography. *Use:* For students of language and linguistics concerned with phonology.

218 Pulgram, Ernst. *Introduction to the Spectography of Speech.* The Hague, Mouton, 1964. 174 p. (Janua linguarum, 7)

Aims to introduce linguists to technical discussions and to the specialized literature of physics and acoustics stressing importance of speech spectography. The four sections deal with: acoustics; phonetics, phonemics; spectrophonetics; spectrophonemics. Bibliography. *Use:* For linguists, phoneticians, acousticians and communication engineers.

219 Trager, George L. and Harry Lee Smith. *An Outline of English Structure.* Washington, American Council of Learned Societies, 1957 [i.e. 1965, c1951] 91 p. (Studies in linguistics: occasional papers, 3)

Aims to present a methodology of scientific analysis of English structure. Emphasis is put on phonology and morphology. Supplied with appendices containing glossary of technical terms and list of symbols and formulas. *Use:* Difficult to follow, this important book is recommended to students in advanced linguistic courses.

220 Trnka, Bohumil. *A Phonological Analysis of Present-Day Standard English.* Rev. new ed. Edited by Tetsuya Kanekiyo & Tamotsu Koizumi. University, Ala., University of Alabama Press [1968, c1966] 155 p. (Alabama linguistic & philological series, 17)

A revised version of the book's 1935 edition, this work accounts for the European and American development in studies on the phonological structure of English language. Deals with phonemes and variants, relevant features of English phonemes, English stress, vowels of unstressed syllables, combination rules, phonological foreignisms, organization of words, the contextual frequency of monosyllabic and disyllabic types, the productivity of phonemes, and the degrees of phonological differentiation of words. Includes bibliography and index. *Use:* For students of linguistics beyond introductory level.

Trubetzkoy, Nikolai S. *Introduction to the Principles of Phonological Descriptions.* Translated by L. A. Murray. Edited by H. Bluhme. The Hague, Martinus Nijhoff, 1968. 46 p. **221**

Originally published as *Anleitung zu phonologischen Beschreibungen*, in 1935, this essay, now translated into English for the first time, summarizes Trubetzkoy's phonology in a set of eleven rules followed by explanations and a treatise on phoneme combinations of prosodic features and boundary signals. It is a work of major importance to the history of phonology. *Use:* For all students of language and linguistics.

Trubetzkoy, Nikolai S. *Principles of Phonology.* Translated by Christiane A. M. Baltaxe. Berkeley, University of California **222** Press, 1969. 344 p.

A new translation of the classic treatise *Grundzuge der Phonologie*, first published in 1938, and considered a final synthesis of phonological ideas and linguistic trends existing before World War II, this is still one of the crucial works in twentieth century European and American linguistics. In addition to the Theory of Distinctiveness and the Theory of Deliminative Elements, the book contains articles on phonology and linguistic geography and on morphonology. Included also are Trubetzkoy's autobiographical notes as related by Roman Jakobson, bibliography of Trubetzkoy's works, and indexes. *Use:* For all linguists and students of linguistics beyond introductory level. *See also* 85, 108, 114, 200.

MORPHOLOGY

Elson, Benjamin and Velma Pickett. *An Introduction to Morphology and Syntax.* [4th ed.] Summer Institute of Linguistics. **223** Santa Ana, Calif., 1965. 167 p.

Meant for student-beginners in linguistics, this is a textbook based on the tagmemic model for language analysis and grammatical descriptions. Divided into five parts it deals with: morphemics; tagmemes and contructions; a survey of construction types; emic units; suggestions for field work. Includes bibliography and index. Supplemented by a separate *Laboratory manual for morphology and syntax,* by W. R. Merrifield and others (Santa Ana, 1962).

224 Nida, Eugene A. *Morphology; the descriptive analysis of words.* 2d ed. Ann Arbor, University of Michigan Press [1963, c1949] 342 p.

Discusses morphological analysis of words into smaller units—morphemes. Treats the morphemes together with their allmorphs as the fundamental feature and does not employ morphological and phonological processes as basic to the descriptive methodology, as it was in the earlier, 1946 edition of the book. Gives examples of actual-language problems to help the student learn about the structure of real languages at the same time as he studies methodology. Includes appendix with supplementary problems and a table of phonetic symbols, bibliography and index. *Use:* Although meant as a text for teaching descriptive linguistics, this book should be used for students in advanced linguistic courses only. *See also* 27, 108, 163, 219,283.

SYNTAX

225 Chomsky, Noam. *Aspects of The Theory of Syntax.* Cambridge, MIT Press [1965] 251 p.

Deals with transformational grammar, stating the author's theory of syntax and that of other linguists. Stress is put on the development of an aspect of generative grammar aiming to simplify the rules of transformation. Includes bibliography, index, and detailed notes to each of the four chapters. *Use:* For those with advanced knowledge of syntax.

Fries, Charles C. *The Structure of English; An Introduction to the Construction of English Sentences.* New York, Harcourt, Brace & World [1952] 304 p.   **226**

A modern grammar of American English, based on recorded conversations. Discusses: kinds of sentences; sentence analysis: meaning or form; parts of speech; function words; parts of speech: formal characteristics; structural patterns of sentences; structural meanings: "subjects" and "objects"; structural meanings: "modifiers"; "sequence" sentences and "included" sentences; and immediate constituents: "layers" of structure. Index.

Langendoen, D. Terence. *The Study of Syntax; the generative-transformational approach to the structure of American English.* New York, Holt, Rinehart and Winston [1969] 174 p.   **227**
(Transatlantic series in linguistics)

Presented in a lucid style, this is an introductory study of basic concepts of modern linguistic theory. The point of view is that of Chomsky's *Aspects of the theory of syntax,* and what may be called a neo-Chomskyan perspective. Reviews of the book are controversial, but most agree that the first three chapters are sound. Supplied with bibliography, glossary, study questions and index. *Use:* Recommended to upper level undergraduates and to graduate students.

Nida, Eugene A. *A Synopsis of English Syntax.* 2d rev. ed. The Hague, Mouton, 1966. 174 p. (Janua linguarum. Series practica, 19)   **228**

The author's doctoral dissertation of 1943, first published in 1960, then revised, this is an important work on structural linguistics oriented toward constructions in terms of immediate constituents. Includes bibliography. *Use:* For specialized linguistic research. *See GRAMMARS. See also* 10, 27, 85, 90, 108, 223, 283.

SEMANTICS

229 Cohen, Laurence J. *The Diversity of Meaning.* [New York] Herder and Herder [1963] 340 p.

Based on some of the author's philosophy lectures at Oxford University, and on reprints of his articles from journals, this book discusses various theories of meaning. Maintains that no single theory of meaning can suit the semantics of all linguists, philosophers, psychologists and translators. Discusses ideas of prominent philosophers concerned with semantics, focusing on works of contemporary thinkers. Includes bibliographical footnotes and index. *Use:* For linguists, philosophers, logicians, and psychologists.

230 Hayakawa, Samuel I. *Language in Thought and Action.* [By] S. I. Hayakawa, in consultation with Leo Hamalian and Geoffrey Wagner. 2d ed. New York, Harcourt, Brace & World [c1964] 350 p.

An introduction to semantics, stressing use of language for communication, written with remarkable clarity and liveliness. Includes bibliography and index. *Use:* For instructors, students of language on all levels and for general readers alike.

231 Hayakawa, S. I., ed. *The Use and Misuse of Language; selections from ETC; a review of general semantics.* Greenwich, Conn., Fawcett Publications [1962] 240 p. (A Premier book, t166)

A selection of essays concerned with the relations between language, thought and behavior. *Use:* Intended for laymen, this is also an informative and entertaining study of semantics for students of language and linguistics.

232 Linsky, Leonard, ed. *Semantics and the Philosophy of Language; A Collection of Readings.* Urbana, University of Illinois Press, 1952. 289 p.

Contains thirteen essays by contemporary philosophers, reprinted from philosophical journals and books. Includes a bibliography. *Use:* Although intended for university students in general, this collection is difficult to understand without previous background in philosophical analysis and symbolic logic.

Ogden, Charles K. and I. A. Richards. *The Meaning of Meaning; a study of the influence of language upon thought and of science of symbolism.* With supplementary essays by B. Malinowski and F. G. Crookshank. New York, Harcourt, Brace & World [1959] 363 p.   **233**

First published in 1923. Written with clarity and humour, this is an important as well as entertaining book on the nature of speech, symbolism and semantics. The supplementary essay by Malinowski on meaning in primitive languages still has value and relevance. Indexes. *Use:* For linguists, ethnologists, grammarians, psychologists and general readers.

Schaff, Adam. *Introduction to Semantics.* Translated from the Polish by Olgierd Wojtasiewicz. Oxford, New York, Pergamon Press [1962] 395 p.   **234**

A comprehensive investigation of the significance and the subject matter of semantics as a branch of linguistics, it is written from a Marxist point of view. Despite its bias, this important work provides for a clear explanation of the difference between linguistic semantics and semantics connected with logic; analyses semantics as the specific philosophical trend, and points out the social and sociological aspects of general semantics. Includes extensive bibliography and index. *Use:* For teachers and students of linguistics, logic and philosophy.

Stern, Gustaf. *Meaning and Change of Meaning, with special reference to the English language.* Bloomington, Indiana University Press [1964, c1931] 456 p. (Indiana University studies in the history and theory of linguistics)   **235**

Presents comprehensive semantic theory based on a study of the historical development of word meaning. Covers language and its function, the definition and analysis of verbal meaning, the production and comprehension of speech, the causes and conditions of sense-changes, transfer, exchanges, and adequation of meaning. Includes bibliography and index of words. Important to linguists and useful to students of psychology.

236 Ullmann, Stephen. *The Principles of Semantics.* [2d ed.] Oxford, Blackwell [1967, c1957] 352 p. (Glasgow University publications, 84)

> Deals with terminology, development, and relationship of semantics with other disciplines, especially with linguistics and philosophy. Separate chapters are devoted to: descriptive semantics, the passage from descriptive to historical semantics, historical semantics, and general semantics. Includes bibliographies and a subject index.

237 Ziff, Paul. *Semantic Analysis.* Ithaca, N. Y., Cornell University Press [1967, c1960] 255 p.

> Philosophical approach to semantic analysis presented on the background of contemporary linguistics, as exemplified on the word "good". Contains bibliography and indexes. *Use:* For instructors and advanced students of language and linguistics. *See also* 85, 108, 176.

STYLISTICS

238 Chatman, Seymour. *A Theory of Meter.* The Hague, Mouton, 1965. 229 p. (Janua linguarum. Series minor, nr. 36)

> Presents application of structural linguistics to the development of a theory of English meter. Discusses: the nature of rhythm; phonological backgrounds to metrical analysis; objective analyses of metrical properties; the components of English meter; Shakespeare's Eighteenth Sonnet: an experiment in metrical analysis; and the function of meter. Appendix deals with the stress systems of Pike and Trager-Smith. Includes bibliographical footnotes. *Use:* For linguists, poets, literary critics and historians, and for all teachers and students concerned with English language, style, poetics, metrics, phonology and phonetics.

Doležel, Lubomir and Richard W. Bailey, eds. *Statistics and Style.*
New York, American Elsevier, 1969. 245 p. (Mathematical **239**
linguistics and automatic language processing, 6)

A collection of essays by statisticians, linguists, psychologists
and literary scholars, aiming to demonstrate the interrelationship between contemporary theories of language and literature and the statistical study of texts. Emphasis is put on a
generative system of language description and a structuralist
conception of literature. Includes articles translated from
French, German and Russian; all grouped into six sections:
the theory of statistical stylistics; vocabulary measures;
sentence-level measures; poetics; individual styles; and history. Contains bibliographical references, notes on the
contributors and index. *Use:* For students in upper level
linguistic courses, for instructors in language and linguistics,
statisticians and literary scholars.

Fowler, Roger, ed. *Essays on Style and Language; linguistic and
critical approaches to literary style.* London, Routledge and K. **240**
Paul [1966] 188 p.

An anthology of writings discussing the literary uses of
language and stylistic analysis in terms of modern linguistic
methods. Includes bibliographical footnotes and index. *Use:*
For all concerned with the study of English literary history
and linguistics.

Freeman, Donald C., ed. *Linguistics and Literary Style.* New
York, Holt, Rinehart and Winston [c1970] 491 p. **241**

Intended for graduate and undergraduate courses in the
combined subjects of modern linguistics and literature, this
collection of reprinted essays presents different approaches
applied to this field by contemporary scholars. Grouped
under five headings the papers discuss: 'Linguistic approaches
to literature' (an introductory chapter by the editor);
'Linguistic stylistics: theory'; 'Linguistic stylistics: method';
'Approaches to prose style'; and 'Approaches to metrics'.
Includes bibliographical notes. *Use:* Recommended to all
concerned with the new trends in linguistics and with the
study and teaching of literary style.

242 Hemphill, George, ed. *Discussions of Poetry: Rhythm and Sound.* Boston, Heath [1961] 112 p. (Discussions of literature)

A chronologically arranged selection of essays on the language of metrical composition. Discusses various aspects of poetry illustrated with representative examples from English and American literary history. Includes writings by Gascoigne, Ben Jonson, Milton, Dryden, Thomas Jefferson, Coleridge, Blake, Hopkins, Saintsbury, Robert Bridges, and others; more recent essays on the sounds of English verse by Harold Whitehall, Seymour Chatman, Arnold Stein and John C. Ransom. *Use:* For all students and teachers of English language and literary history.

243 Hough, Graham. *Style and Stylistics.* London, Routledge & K. Paul. New York, Humanities Press [1969] 114 p. (Concepts of literature)

Gives a brief account of modern research on literary style and investigates linguistic contributions to the study of literature. Provides critical evaluation of terms associated with stylistics, giving references to most illustrative poetic and prose works in literary history. Concludes pointing out the relationship of literature to other disciplines: anthropology, philosophy and psychology. Includes a bibliography. *Use:* For all concerned with the study and teaching of literary style, modern languages and linguistics.

244 Leech, Geoffrey N. *A Linguistic Guide to English Poetry.* [London] Longmans [1969] 240 p. (English language series)

Intended as an introductory course in stylistics for undergraduate students in English, this book provides an interpretation of literature employing linguistic methods which require no specialized knowledge. Emphasizes that the linguistic and critical aspects of literary studies are regarded in this work as complementary, and that poetic language is related to other uses of the English language and art forms. Includes chapters on: poetic tradition, creative uses of language, poetic licence, characteristic features of poetic language (e.g. verbal repetition), patterns of sound, metre and rhythm, use of rhetorical figures and meaning, ambiguity and multiple interpretations. Contains examples for dicussion following each chapter; suggestions for further reading;

general index; and an index of sources of examples for discussion.

Levin, Samuel R. *Linguistic Structures in Poetry*. The Hague, Mouton, 1969. 64 p. (Janua linguarum. Studia memoriae Nicolai van Wijk dedicata, 23)   **245**

The book makes a major contribution to linguistics and literary theory with that it describes what the author calls "coupling", a structure that appears in the language of poetry and functions as a unifying device. Attempts to provide explanation for two responses to poetry: that it is unified and that it is memorable (permanent). Devotes separate chapters to: poetry, grammar, stylistics; paradigms and positions; coupling; the conventional matrix; and a sonnet. Includes a bibliography. *Use:* For students of language and linguistics in upper level undergraduate and graduate courses.

Martin, Harold C., ed. *Style in Prose Fiction*. New York, Columbia University Press [c1957] 209 p. [English Institute.   **246** Essays, 1958]

An important collection of essays, reprinted from the English Institute Meetings of 1957 and 1958, discussing various approaches to the stylistic analysis; presented in the light of modern research in language. Examples are drawn from both English and American fiction. Included is an excellent bibliography compiled by Harold C. Martin and Richard M. Ohmann. *Use:* Recommended especially to students of English language and literary history.

Nowottny, Winifred. *The Language Poets Use*. New York, Oxford University Press, 1962. 225 p.   **247**

Based on lectures delivered to students of English at the University of London, this book discusses the nature of poetry in relation to language and the diversity of interaction between words and meanings. Includes sections on: elements of poetic language; diction; metaphor and poetic structure; schematization and abstraction; ambiguity; symbolism and obscurity. Contains much detailed criticism of individual poems. Includes bibliographical footnotes and index. *Use:* For all students and teachers of English language and linguistics, literary historians and critics.

248 Sebeok, Thomas A., ed. *Style in Language.* [Cambridge] Technology Press of Massachusetts Institute of Technology [1960] 470 p.

Contains a collection of papers presented at the first interdisciplinary Conference on Style, held at Indiana University in 1958, including contributions by leading literary critics, linguists, psychologists and anthropologists. Focuses on the nature and characteristics of style in literature. Papers are grouped into nine sections, dealing with poetic process and literary analysis, style in folk literature, linguistic appraoches to verbal art, phonological, metrical, grammatical, semantic and psychological aspects of style. Following each section are comments of the Conference's participants. Included also are biographical notes, bibliographical references, and index. *Use:* Very readable; recommended to all concerned with the style in language.

249 Spencer, John W., ed. *Linguistics and Style.* London, Oxford University Press, 1964. 109 p. (Language and language learning, 6)

Contents.—On defining style: an essay in applied linguistics [by] Nils Erik Enkvist.—An appraoch to the study of style [by] John Spencer [and] Michael Gregory.

Both monographs deal with the relationship between literary studies and modern linguistics. The volume includes a brief, but excellent bibliography. *Use:* For teachers and students of English at university and upper high school levels.

250 Thomas, Owen P. *Metaphor, and Related Subjects.* Consulting editor: Richard Ohmann. New York, Random House [1969] 85 p.

An important study of the nature, mechanics and use's of metaphor, based on recent linguistic developments. Examines the process of definition underlying all metaphorical expression, and focuses on the unity which gives meaning to the variety of forms. Supplied with examples from well-known literary works. Includes exercises after each chapter. Bibliography. *Use:* For all students of the English language. *See also* 9, 18.

PSYCHOLINGUISTICS

Brown, Roger. *Words and Things.* Free Press [1968, c1958]
398 p.   **251**

An introduction to language, presented in terms of structural
linguistics, psychology of linguistic behavior, and anthropology. Discusses: the sound system of the language; relation
between thought, speech and writing; nature of meaning;
language of animals; phonetic symbolism and linguistic
relativity; language pathology; mass control by propaganda;
and problems of psychological measurements. Bibliography.
Index. *Use:* Written in a lucid style, this book is recommended to all student beginners in language and linguistics,
psychology, anthropology, and to general readers.

Carroll, John B. *Language and Thought.* Prentice-Hall, Englewood
Cliffs, N. J. [1964] 118 p. (Foundations of modern psychology   **252**
series)

An introductory approach to the psychology of language.
Deals with: language and communication; the nature of
language; the learning of language; aspects of language
behavior; individual differences in language behavior; cognition and thinking; language and cognition. Includes a brief
bibliography and an index. *Use:* For students in linguistics,
social and biological sciences.

Chomsky, Noam. *Language and Mind.* New York, Harcourt,
Brace & World, 1968. 88 p.   **253**

An expanded version of three lectures delivered by the
author at the University of California, Berkeley, in 1967,
discussing linguistic contributions to the study of mind in the
past, present and future. Bibliographical notes. *Use:* Clearly
presented, this is an important and interesting work, recommended to all concerned with linguistics, psychology, behavioral and social sciences and education.

254 De Cecco, John P., ed. *The Psychology of Language, Thought, and Instruction; readings.* New York, Holt, Rinehart and Winston [1967] 446 p.

A collection of writings by prominent linguists and psychologists, discussing current trends in linguistics and focusing on interrelations of language, thought and education. Supplied with editor's introductions to each chapter; bibliographical references; tables, diagrams; index. *Use:* For students and teachers of language linguistics, psychologists, anthropologists and sociologists.

255 Dixon, Theodore R. and David L. Horton, eds. *Verbal Behavior and General Behavior Theory.* Englewood Cliffs, N. J., Prentice-Hall [1968] 596 p. (Prentice-Hall psychology series)

Collection of twenty-four papers by specialists on psychological aspects of verbal behavior, presented at the 1966 Conference, University of Kentucky. The proceedings are divided into five parts. The first four deal with: associative processes, learning and retention, related processes and psycholinguistics. Part 5 contains three discussion papers. Included is an appendix: 'A formal limitation of associationism', prepared especially for this volume. The papers focus on verbal behavior and its relation to general stimulus-response (S-R) theory. Index; bibliography; diagrams; tables. *Use:* For linguists, psychologists and educators.

256 Jakobovits, Leon A. and Murray S. Miron, eds. *Readings in the Psychology of Language.* Englewood-Cliffs, N. J., Prentice-Hall, 1967. 637 p. (Prentice-Hall psychology series)

Collection of 35 papers on the subject of psycholinguistics, written mostly during the past decade. Grouped into three parts: 'Theoretical formulations', 'Experimental approaches to languages', and 'The problem of meaning'. Each section is prefaced with an introduction in which the editors explain the differences in views of psychologists and linguists on topics of common interest. *Use:* Recommended to all students of language and linguistics, psychologists, logicians, teachers of speech and communication engineers.

84

Lenneberg, Eric H., ed. *New Directions in the Study of Language.* Cambridge, MIT Press [1964] 194 p.   **257**

Contains several papers presented at the 17th International Congress of Psychology, held in Washington in 1963. Papers deal with interdisciplinary topics, concerning language problems in relatiori to social anthropology, human biology, experimental psychology, and acquisition of speech. Included are excellent bibliographical references and index. *Use:* Written in a non-technical style, it is recommended to students of language and linguistics at all levels, psychologists, anthropologists, administrators, consultants and advisors.

Lyons, J. and R. J. Wales, eds. *Psycholinguistic Papers:* the proceedings of the 1966 Edinburgh Conference. Edinburgh,   **258** University Press [c1966] 243 p.

A collection of papers including: on hearing sentences: organization of linguistic performance; creation of language by children; some reflections on competence and performance; and syntactic regularities in the speech of children. The papers are followed by discussions. Bibliography and index of names. *Use:* For linguists, psychologists and educators.

Osgood, Charles E. and Thomas A. Sebeok, eds. *Psycholinguistics; A Survey of Theory and Research Problems.* With A survey of   **259** psycholinguistic research, 1954-1964, by A. Richard Diebold and The psycholinguists, by George A. Miller. Bloomington, Indiana University Press [1965] 307 p. (Indiana University studies in the history and theory of linguistics)

Based on the program of the Summer Seminar of Psycholinguistics held at Indiana University in 1953, the material is presented in three sections: psycholinguistics, a survey of theory and research problems; a survey of psycholinguistic research, 1954-1964, and an appendix, the psycholinguistics, on the new scientists of language. Contains extensive bibliographical notes. *Use:* Important to linguists and psychologists.

260 Saporta, Sol, ed. *Psycholinguistics; A Book of Reading.* Prepared with the assistance of Jarvis R. Bastian. New York, Holt, Rinehart and Winston [c1961] 551 p.

Arranged in eight sections, it is a collection of reprints from books and journals dealing with: nature and function of language; approaches to the study of language, speech perception, sequential organization of linguistic events; semantic aspects of linguistic events; language acquisition, bilingualism, and language change; pathologies of linguistic behavior; linguistic relativity and the relation of linguistic processes to perception and cognition. Contains bibliographies; tables, charts, diagrams. *Use:* Meant to facilitate interdisciplinary communication between psychologists and linguists.

261 Skinner, Burrhus F. *Verbal Behavior.* New York, Appleton-Century-Crofts [1957] 478 p.

A comprehensive study of language presented from the view point of behavioristic psychology stressing the stimulus and response factors. Includes index. *Use:* For linguists and psychologists.

262 Smith, Frank and George A. Miller, eds. *The Genesis of Language: a psycholinguistic approach.* Cambridge, Mass., M.I.T. Press [1966] 400 p.

The proceedings of a conference on 'Language development in children', sponsored by the National Institute of Child Health and Human Development, National Institutes of Health, in 1965. Deals with various stages of the acquisition of grammar and phonology by children, and covers such topics as developmental psycholinguistics, the development of the phonological system in the normal and the deaf child, evolutionary aspects of language development, parallels between animal communication and prelinguistic child behavior and other subjects. Included are bibliographical references; appendix: 'Soviet methods of investigating child language' and 'Abstracts of Soviet studies of child language'; and index. *Use:* For linguists, psychologists, behavioral scientists and educators.

Vygotsky, Lev S. *Thought and Language*. Edited and translated by Eugenia Hanfmann and Gertrude Vakar. Cambridge, Mass., **263** MIT Press [1965, c1962] 168 p.

First published in Russian in 1934, and translated into English in 1962, this is a study of the interrelation of thought and speech in the intellectual development of children. Discusses the theories of outstanding psychologists, especially those of Piaget and Stern. Includes bibliography and index. *Use:* Good source of references for linguists, psychologists, educators and interested laymen. *See also* 32, 82, 103, 108.

SOCIOLINGUISTICS

Boas, Franz. *Race, Language and Culture*. New York, Free Press [1966, c1940] 647 p. **264**

Collection of over sixty papers written by the author between 1891 and 1937. Besides the topics covering anthropology, ethnology, mythology, art, religion, etc., there are essays devoted to American Indian languages. *Use:* Valuable to teachers and students of social sciences and linguistics.

Bright, William, ed. *Sociolinguistics;* proceedings of the UCLA Sociolinguistics Conference, 1964. Mouton, 1966. 324 p. **265** (Janua linguarum. Series maior, 20)

Contains fourteen interesting papers and tape-recorded discussions on various aspects of sociolinguistics, as revised for publication by the participants of the Conference (as above), and by the editor.

Capell, Arthur. *Studies in Socio-linguistics.* The Hague, Mouton, 1966. 167 p. (Janua linguarum. Series minor, 46) **266**

Presents various aspects of interrelationship of linguistics, anthropology and sociology, including linguistic acculturation, kinship language, class languages and problems of national languages in multilanguage nations. Contains a bibliography; no index. *Use:* For students and instructors in linguistics, sociology and anthropology.

267 Fishman, Joshua A., ed. *Readings in the Sociology of Language.* The Hague, Mouton, 1968. 808 p.

Important and interesting collection of papers by contemporary linguists. Following an introductory chapter by the editor, there are seven sections: perspective on the sociology of language; language in small-group interactions; language in social strata and sectors; language reflections of socio-cultural organization; multilingualism; language maintenance and language shift; the social contexts and consequences of language planning. Includes bibliographies; name and subject indexes. *Use:* Book meant especially for instructors and students.

268 Greenberg, Joseph H. *Anthropological Linguistics; an introduction.* New York, Random House [1968] 212 p.

Written in a nontechnical style, this book deals with the nature and definition of language, linguistics as a science, descriptive linguistics, grammatical theory, phonology, linguistic change, types of language classification, synchronic universals, diachronic generalization, and higher-level explanations. Contains notes with bibliographical references, a list of symbols, and index. *Use:* For both graduate and undergraduate students of linguistics and anthropology.

269 Labov, William. *The Social Stratification of English in New York City.* [Washington] Center for Applied Linguistics, 1966. 655 p.

Originally a Ph.D. dissertation, this is an extensive linguistic analysis of various socio-economic groups in New York City. Based on a survey of over a hundred and twenty department store employees, it gives a cross section of the New York speech community and identifies the socio-linguistic norms used within that community. Includes table of contents, bibliography, glossary of linguistic symbols and terminology, appendices, charts and diagrams, but no index.

Samarin, William J. *Field Linguistics; A Guide to Linguistic Field Work.* New York, Holt, Rinehart and Winston, 1967. 246 p.   **270**

Stress is put on the collection of linguistic data and methods of finding and training of native informants, especially those in a lesser known language. Much attention is devoted to acquisition and use of various tools for recording, processing and presenting the results. *Use:* Important book, designed primarily for the linguistic field workers, but useful also to dialectologists, ethnographers and general interested readers.

Sapir, Edward. *Culture, Language and Personality;* selected essays edited by David G. Mandelbaum. [1st paper-bound ed.]   **271** Berkeley, University of California Press, 1964 [c1949] 207 p.

Contains nine essays chosen from the larger collection, entitled *Selected Writings of Edward Sapir in Language, Culture and Personality,* published in 1949. The essays discuss various aspects of language and linguistics, genetic affiliations among languages, relations between language and the rest of a culture, and interaction of culture and personality. *Use:* Essential to all linguists, psychologists, sociologists and anthropologists. *See also* 23, 108, 109, 113.

COMPUTATIONAL LINGUISTICS

Akhmanova, O. S. *Exact Methods in Linguistic Research.* [By] O. S. Akhmanova [and others] Translated from the Russian by   **272** David G. Hays and Dolores V. Mohr. Berkeley, University of California Press, 1963. 186 p.

Among the best Russian works on computational aspects of their science, this is a collection of papers dealing with fundamental definitions and problems in linguistics. Discussed are the uses of the term "semantics" and analyzed the terms "grammatical" and "syntactic". Stress is put on the application of mathematical techniques to the problems posed in the book. Much attention is centred on introductions to statistics and information theory and to machine translation. Includes bibliographies and index.

273 Freeman, Robert R., Alfred Pietrzyk and A. Hood Roberts, eds. *Information in the Language Sciences.* New York, American Elsevier, 1968. 247 p. (Mathematical linguistics and automatic language processing, 5)

"Proceedings of the Conference held at Airlie House, Warrenton, Virginia, March 4-6, 1966, under the sponsorship of the Center for Applied Linguistics." An important collection of papers presented at the Airlie House Conference emphasizing three main themes: "General trends" (rapid increase in the amount and degree of organization of scientific research, increasing amounts of recorded information and the scholars' demands for instant access, interdependence or merging of various areas that deal with communication and control of information); "Information needs of the language sciences" (outline of the flow of information in linguistics); and "System design" (current information services). Included are very useful bibliographical references and diagrams, summaries of discussions, list of conference participants, and index. *Use:* For linguists, behaviorists, social scientists, system analysts, and computer specialists.

274 Garvin, Paul L. *On Linguistic Method; selected papers.* The Hague, Mouton, 1964. 158 p. (Janua linguarum. Series minor, nr. 30)

A collection of papers dealing with descriptive method in linguistics and in some aspects of language-and-culture research. Covers: phonemics, morphology, syntax, meaning, language and culture. *Use:* For specialized linguistic research.

275 Garvin, Paul L. and Bernard Spolsky, eds. *Computation in Linguistics; a case book.* Bloomington, Indiana University Press [1966] 332 p. (Indiana University studies in the history and theory of linguistics)

Contains twelve papers—case studies exemplifying various degrees of computer participation in several fields of linguistics. The papers, originally presented at the 1964 Summer Linguistic Institute at Indiana University, are organized in terms of the two fundamental capabilities of the computer: data processing problems and systems problems. The former deal with descriptive, historical and dialect data; the latter discuss descriptive problems in phonology, morphology and syntax, and applied problems in machine translation, content processing, and programmed instruction. Included are numerous diagrams and tables. *Use:* For teachers and students of languages and linguistics beyond introductory level; for computer programmers, systems analysts and communication engineers.

Hays, David G. *Introduction to Computational Linguistics,* New York, American Elsevier [1967] 231 p. (Mathematical linguistics and automatic language processing, 2)   **276**

Meant as a basic course textbook for university students who have no previous experience with computational linguistics, this work discusses the computer and then proceeds from superficial to the most difficult topics. There are exercises and bibliographical references following each of the thirteen chapters. Included is a list of computer instructions and index. *Use:* For students of computational linguistics, linguists, computer specialists and managers.

Hays, David G., ed. *Readings in Automatic Language Processing.* New York, American Elsevier, 1966. 202 p.   **277**

A collection of papers dealing with methods, solutions to central problems, or approaches to the use of the computer as a processor of natural language. Includes chapters on high-speed large-capacity dictionary system, connectability calculations, syntactic functions, and Russian syntax, research methodology for machine translation, keyword-in-context index for technical literature, and a framework for syntactic translation, among other topics. Includes tables, diagrams, bibliographical references and index. *Use:* For linguists, students of linguistics beyond introductory level, computer programmers and systems analysts.

Ortiz, Alejandro and Ernesto Zierer. *Set Theory and Linguistics.* The Hague, Mouton, 1968. 61 p. (Janua linguarum. Series minor, nr. 70)   **278**

Aims to promote interest in the potential importance of modern algebra in linguistics. Presents material discussed at the 1965 seminar, organized by the Department of Foreign Languages and Linguistics at the National University of Trujillo, Peru, and follows its study sessions' arrangement.

Devotes one part to the explanation of the mathematical theory involved, and the other to its application to linguistic phenomena. Includes a selected bibliography. *Use:* For linguists and students of linguistics concerned with the use of mathematics in linguistic research. *See also* 16, 82, 108

TRANSLATION

279 Arrowsmith, William & Roger Shattuck, eds. *The Craft and Context of Translation, a symposium.* Austin, Published by University of Texas Press for Humanities Research Center [1961] 206 p.

A collection of essays, in Part One—delivered at a Symposium on Translation, at the University of Texas in 1959—considers translation as a fine art and a cultural force; in Part Two, added later, deals with the role of the editor; the status of the full time professional translator; and translation as a political instrument. The last part consists of an addenda of translation in Latin, Greek, and six modern European languages. *Use:* Intended for translators, editors and publishers, recommended to all students of modern languages.

280 Catford, John C. *A Linguistic Theory of Translation; an Essay in Applied Linguistics.* London, Oxford University Press, 1965. 103 p. (Language and language learning, 8)

Based on lectures given in the School of Applied Linguistics at Edinburgh University, this book deals with various problems of translation and sets up a theory of translation. First chapter, addressed to the general reader, discusses the nature of language and the categories of general linguistics. *Use:* For language-teachers, students of linguistics, professional and amateur translators, and general interested readers.

Nida, Eugene A. *Toward a Science of Translating, with special reference to principles and procedures involved in Bible translating.* Leiden, E. J. Brill, 1964. 331 p.   281

Discusses principles, problems and techniques involved in the process of translation. Deals with phonological, morphological, syntactical, lexical, stylistic, and other factors existing between source and translation. Gives detailed analysis of problems posed by morphological categories. Devotes final chapter to the implications of machine translation in practice and theory. Includes extensive bibliography and index. *Use:* Considered one of the best books in the field published in recent years, it is strongly recommended to translators, linguists and anthropologists.

STUDY AND TEACHING

Bennett, William A. *Aspects of Language and Language Teaching.* Cambridge, University Press [1968] 175 p.   282

Discusses principles of transformational-generative grammar and systemic grammar. Emphasises the use of new methods in language teaching and learning; points out the underlying linguistic and psychological theories. Stresses the importance of audio-visual materials and the language laboratory. Contains numerous illustrations, bibliography, glossary, and index. *Use:* Recommended to all teachers and students of language and linguistics.

Bloch, Bernard and George L. Trager. *Outline of Linguistic Analysis.* Baltimore, Md., Pub. by Linguistic Society of America at the Waverly Press, 1942. 82 p. (Special publications of the Linguistic Society of America)   283

A concise introduction to the techniques of linguistic analysis and to the scientific attitude toward language-learning. Aims to assist those studying a foreign language by the method of working with native speakers and arriving inductively at the grammatical system of their language. Deals with: language and linguistics, phonetics, phonemics, morphology, and syntax. Includes a reading list. *Use:* For teachers of language, students of language and linguistics at all levels, and for educated laymen.

284 Brooks, Nelson. *Language and Language Learning; theory and practice.* 2d ed. New York, Harcourt, Brace & World [1964] 300 p.

Intended primarily as an aid to foreign-language teachers, this is a comprehensive book in presenting various aspects of modern teaching methods. Deals with language theory, acquisition of a second language, language learning and teaching, language and culture, language and literature, teaching materials, laboratory exercises, and tests and measurements. Includes glossary of terms, bibliographies and index. *Use:* Important to instructors in modern languages and English; useful to university students at all levels.

285 Carroll, John B. *The Study of Language; A Survey of Linguistics and Related Disciplines in America.* Cambridge, Harvard University Press [1963, c1953] 289 p.

Interesting, and still useful, survey of various approaches to the study of language and linguistics. Deals with: the science of linguistics; linguistics and psychology; linguistics and the social sciences; linguistics and philosophy; language and education; communication engineering and the study of speech; organizations, personnel and publications; the future of language studies. Contains extensive notes; bibliography; index.

286 Emig, Janet A., James T. Fleming and Helen M. Popp, eds. *Language and Learning.* New York, Harcourt, Brace & World [1966] 301 p.

Collection of articles from *The Harvard Educational Review,* focusing on several aspects of language learning; to name a few: child's acquisition of syntax, development of children's speech and language disorders, grammar analysis and the use

94

of English in world literature. Includes bibliographical references and index. *Use:* For teachers and students of language and linguistics at all levels, for psychologists and general interested readers.

Halliday, M. A. K., Angus McIntosh and Peter Strevens. *The Linguistic Sciences and Language Teaching.* Bloomington,   **287**
Indiana University Press [1965, c1964] 322 p. (Indiana University studies in the history and theory of linguistics)

Important book, presenting the role of linguistics in various aspects of language teaching and learning. Divided into two parts it deals, in part 1, with the principles of language description, comparison and translation; focuses on relevance of linguistic and phonetic theory to a number of language problems. Part 2 discusses application of linguistic research to the native and foreign teaching. Includes bibliography and index. *Use:* Meant especially for language teachers, textbook writers and school administrators; recommended to all students of language and linguistics.

Lado, Robert. *Linguistics Across Cultures; Applied Linguistics for Language Teachers.* With a foreword by Charles C. Fries. Ann   **288**
Arbor, University of Michigan Press [1964, c1957] 141 p.

Presents the "new approach" to teaching and learning of a foreign language, based on a systematic linguistic-cultural comparison of the student's native language with the language he wants to learn. Shows the significance of a careful descriptive analysis of sound systems, grammatical structures and vocabulary systems. Includes diagrams, table of phonetic and phonemic symbols, general bibliographical information and a selected bibliography.

Mackey, William F. *Language Teaching Analysis.* [London]   **289**
Longmans, 1965. 554 p.

Discusses various aspects of language analysis, planning, testing and technique of teaching. Includes extensive topical bibliography; appendixes on language drills and games; tables, diagrams; index. *Use:* Detailed but excellent book for language teachers, researchers and students.

290   Moulton, William G. *A Linguistic Guide to Language Learning.* [New York] Modern Language Association of America, 1966. 140 p.

Written in a simple language, this is a very useful book dealing with principles of general and contrastive linguistics. Meant for both students and teachers. Includes appendix with a short annotated bibliography and a subject index.

291   Palmer, Harold E. *The Principles of Language-Study.* London, Oxford University Press [1964] 142 p. (Language and language learning, 5)

A reprint of the 1921 publication, now a classic study on the theory and practice of learning and teaching of a language. *Use:* For teachers, students and general readers alike.

292   Palmer, Harold E. *The Scientific Study and Teaching of Language.* Ed. by David Harper. London, Oxford University Press, 1968. 236 p. (Language and language learning, 18)

First published in 1917, this companion volume, or an introduction to *The principles of language-study,* is still useful in presenting various aspects of learning and successful teaching technique. Includes list of phonetic symbols, ergonic chart and glossary of technical terms. Index. *Use:* For teachers, students and interested general readers.

293   Strevens, Peter. *Papers in Language and Language Teaching.* London, Oxford University Press, 1965. 152 p. (Language and language learning, 9)

Collection of twelve reprinted essays by the author, dealing with linguistic research, phonetics, applied linguistics and language teaching. *Use:* Valuable to students and teachers concerned with modern developments in language teaching and linguistic sciences.

294   Sweet, Henry. *The Practical Study of Languages; A Guide for Teachers and Learners.* London, Oxford University Press, 1964. 276 p. (Language and language learning, 1)

First published in 1899, this is a classic of still current interest dealing with theory and practice of the teaching and learning of languages. Discusses: phonetics, grammar, orthography, the spoken language, principles of method, text, composition, research, and mind-training in classical and modern languages. *See also* 7, 11, 14, 20, 21, 22, 25, 29, 30, 32, 108, 241, 253, 255, 262.

II

LINGUISTIC PERIODICALS AND SERIES

Acta Linguistica Hafniensia. Copenhagen. v. 9, 1965- . **295**

Volumes 1-8 entitled: "Acta Linguistica: Revue Internationale de Linguistique Structurale". An international semi-annual journal of structural linguistics published under the auspieces of the Linguistic Circle of Copenhagen. Contains articles and book reviews in English, French and German. Indexed in *Linguistic Bibliography,* and in *Language and Language Behavior Abstracts.*

American Speech. New York. v. 1, 1925- . **296**

"A Quarterly of Linguistic Usage", published by Columbia University with contributions from other leading American universities. Contains scholarly articles, notes on proceedings of international congresses, bibliographies and book reviews. Interesting feature "Among the new words", a section devoted to neologisms in English (American) language. Index in December issue. Indexed in *Social Sciences & Humanities Index,* also in *Language and Language Behavior Abstracts.*

Anthropological Linguistics. Bloomington, Ind. v. 1, 1959- . **297**

Issued nine times a year by the Archives of Languages of the World, Anthropology Department, Indiana University. Meant chiefly to assist scholars by immediate publication of the data from tape recordings available on deposit in the Archives. Contains theoretical and methodological papers on special problems in phonemics, morphonemics, morphemics, syntax and comparative grammar. Includes lexical lists and analyzed texts, charts, diagrams; detailed index to languages of the world in vol. 8, 1966. Indexed in *Linguistic Bibliography*, also in *Annual Bibliography of English Language and Literature.*

298   *Archivum Linguisticum.* Glasgow. v. 1, 1949- .

"A Review of Comparative Philology and General Linguistics", which appears in two fascicules a year. Published by the University of Glasgow, chiefly in English and French, but also in German, Italian and Spanish. Contains scholarly articles and book reviews relating to both ancient and modern languages. Indexed in *The Year's Work in Modern Language Studies,* and in *Language and Language Behavior Abstracts.*

299   *Babel.* Paris. v. 1, 1955- .

International quarterly journal devoted to information and research in the field of translation. Includes book reviews, bibliographies, and lists of translators. Text in French, English and German. Indexed in *MLA International Bibliography,* also in *Language and Language Behavior Abstracts.*

300   *Canadian Journal of Linguistics.* Toronto v. 1, 1955- .

Semi-annual publication of the Canadian Linguistic Association, compiled and issued by the University of Toronto. Aims to promote the scientific study of language and languages, particularly of the written and spoken languages of Canada. Text in English and French. Annual bibliographies and supplements for previous years entitled *Linguistica Canadiana.* Contains book reviews and announcements of new publications. Cumulative author index, 1961-65. Indexed in *Annual Bibliography of English Language and Literature,* also in *Linguistic Bibliography.*

301   *Canadian Modern Language Review.* Toronto. v. 1, 1964- .

Quarterly journal of the Ontario Modern Language Teachers' Association. Although intended primarily for teachers, it may be used by students of modern languages. Contains feature articles on methods of teaching and learning, sample exercises for classroom use, junior and senior high school levels, book

102

reviews; notes of interest, charts, indexes. Text in English, French, German, Italian, Russian and Spanish. Indexed in *MLA International Bibliography,* also in *Language and Language Behavior Abstracts.*

Etc. San Francisco. v. 1, 1943- .   **302**

Quarterly review of general semantics, it is an "official organ of the International Society for General Semantics, for the encouragement of scientific research and theoretical inquiry into nonaristotelian systems and general semantics". Concerned with the role of language and symbols in human behavior. Includes book reviews, correspondence and notes on discussions arising from recent publications. Indexes. Indexed in *Annual Bibliography of English Language and Literature,* and in *Psychological Abstracts.*

Folia Linguistica. The Hague, Mouton. v. 1, 1967- .   **303**

Subtitle: "Acta Societatis Linguisticae Europaeae". Published in two double issues per year, in English, French, German and Russian. Intends to contribute to the advancement of the scientific research on language in all its aspects, emphasizing European studies. Indexed in *The Year's Work in Modern Language Studies* and in *Language and Language Behavior Abstracts.*

Forum for Modern Language Studies. Fife, Scotland. v. 1, 1965- . **304**

Quarterly publication of the University of St. Andrews, Scotland, attempting to cover "the principal languages and literatures of Europe and America during the past millenium", and to avoid "studies showing a narrowly specialized approach or on topics of little general interest."—Edit. Contains book reviews and advertisements. Indexed in *Annual Bibliography of English Language and Literature,* also in *MLA International Bibliography.*

Foundations of Language. Dordrecht, The Netherlands. v. 1,   **305**
1965- .

Quarterly. The subtitle "International Journal of Language and Philosophy" determines the scope of this publication, devoted to studies on the foundations of language and its relations with various disciplines. Contains book reviews, discussions arising from recent publications and indexes of names. Text in English, occasionally in German and French. Indexed in *The Year's Work in Modern Language Studies,* also in *Language and Language Behavior Abstracts.*

306 *General Linguistics.* University Park, Pa. v. 1, 1955- .

Published three times a year by the Pennsylvania State University. Contains articles and book reviews in the fields of historical, comparative and descriptive linguistics as well as in the related fields of psycholinguistics and sociolinguistics. Text in English, French, German and Russian. Indexed in *Annual Bibliography of English Language and Literature,* also in *MLA International Bibliography.*

307 *General Semantics Bulletin.* Lakeville, Conn. no. 1, 1949- .

Irregular. Published for 'Members of the Institute' by the Institute of General Semantics, Lakeville, Conn. Meant "for information and intercommunication among workers in the non-aristotelian discipline formulated by Alfred Korzybski". Deals with the scientific epistemologic backgrounds of general semantics, orientations in modern neuropsycho-physiology, psychotherapy, education, etc. Includes notes on conferences; discussions; book reviews. Author and key-word-in-title indexes to the first 33 nos. in Feb. 1968 issue.

308 GEORGETOWN UNIVERSITY, Washington, D. C. Institute of Languages and Linguistics. *Monograph Series on Languages and Linguistics.* no. 1, 1951- .

309 GEORGETOWN UNIVERSITY, Washington, D. C. Institute of Languages and Linguistics. *Report of the Annual Round Table Meeting on Linguistics and Language Studies.*

Subseries of the *Monograph Series on Languages and Linguistics,* containing texts of papers presented at meetings, and discussions which followed them. Editor, chairman of the Annual Round Table Meeting, varies from year to year.

Above series are the publications of the Institute of Language and Linguistics (established by the School of Foreign Service at Georgetown University in 1949), aiming "to bring together what may be called the more traditional language teachers and representatives of the newer school of scientific linguistics, especially descriptive linguistics. Another point of particular emphasis is consideration of the use of new technological aids for language".–Pref. to No. 1, Sept., 1951.

Glossa. Burnaby, B. C. v. 1, 1967- .   **310**

Published semi-annually by the Glossa Society, Department of Modern Languages, Simon Fraser University. Devoted to linguistic theory and language description; includes psycholinguistics, sociolinguistics, mathematical, and anthropological linguistics. Contains book reviews. For highly specialized linguistic research. Indexed in *Language and Language Behavior Abstracts.*

INTERNATIONAL CONGRESS OF LINGUISTS. *Proceedings.*   **311**
1928- .

Title varies: Actes or Acti. Published at irregular intervals by different editors and publishers. Contributions in English, French, German, or Italian.

INTERNATIONAL CONGRESS OF PHONETIC SCIENCES.   **312**
Proceedings. 1932- .

Published at irregular intervals by different editors and publishers. Contributions in English, French and German.

International Journal of American Linguistics. Baltimore. v. 1,   **313**
1927- .

Quarterly. Published by Indiana University under the auspices of Linguistic Society of America and American Anthropological Association. Specializes in American Indian languages. Includes scholarly articles on typological classification. Contains book reviews, charts, indexes; cumulative index every 10 years. Indexed in *MLA International Bibliography,* also in *Social Sciences & Humanities Index.*

314 *Iral: International Review of Applied Linguistics in Language Teaching.* Heidelberg. v. 1, 1963- .

Quarterly scholarly publication devoted to problems of general and applied linguistics in all their aspects. Contains book reviews, bibliographies, advertisements, indexes. Text in English, French and German. Indexed in *Linguistic Bibliography*, also in *MLA International Bibliography*.

315 JANUA LINGUARUM. *Studia Memoriae Nicolai Van Wijk Dedicata. Series Minor.* The Hague. v. 1, 1956- .

316 JANUA LINGUARUM. *Studia Memoriae Nicolai Van Wijk Dedicata. Series Maior.* The Hague. v. 1, 1959- .

Both of the above are series of monographs dealing with grammar, speech and other aspects of language, emphasizing trends in modern linguistics, and reporting on the proceedings of international congresses. *Series Minor* include publications smaller in size; they average from some sixty to two hundred pages. *Series Maior* are larger, often multi-volume scholarly works, such as the three volume set *To Honor Roman Jakobson.*

317 *Journal of English Linguistics.* Bellingham, Wash. v. 1, 1967- .

Issued in an annual volume of one number, in March, by English Department, Western Washington State College. Devoted exclusively to the English language in its historical and modern periods. Discusses all dialects and world varieties of English. Includes scholarly book reviews, linguistic maps, charts, and detailed analyses of selected words. Indexed in *Language-Teaching Abstracts.*

318 *Journal of Linguistics.* Cambridge. v. 1, 1965- .

Semi-annual, published for the Linguistics Association of Great Britain by Cambridge University. (American branch in New York) Deals with both theoretical and applied linguistics. Reports on research papers in progress. Carries book reviews, and discussions arising from recent publications. Recruits contributors from linguists in all countries. Text mainly in English but also in French, German and Russian; Greek and IPA types used occasionally. Indexed in *The*

Year's Work in Modern Language Studies and in *MLA International Bibliography.*

Journal of Speech and Hearing Disorders. Washington, D. C. **319**
v. 13, 1948- .

Previously *Journal of Speech Disorders* (v. 1, 1936–v. 12, 1947). Quarterly publication of the American Speech and Hearing Association dealing with speech pathology and audiology, evaluation and remedial procedures, counselling, etc. Contains bibliographies, book reviews, indexes; tables, charts, diagrams. Indexed in *Education Index, Language and Language Behavior Abstracts, Psychological Abstracts, Biological Abstracts.*

Journal of Verbal Learning and Verbal Behavior. New York. v. 1, **320**
1962- .

Bi-monthly publication of American Psychological Association. Contains articles, major papers, critical notes, and supplementary reports, dealing with experimental and theoretical problems of verbal learning, human memory, psycholinguistics, and other closely related verbal processes. Includes bibliographies, author and subject indexes, illustrations, charts, diagrams, etc. Indexed in *Linguistic Bibliography, MLA International Bibliography, Psychological Abstracts,* also in *Language and Language Behavior Abstracts.*

Language. Baltimore. v. 1, 1925- . **321**

Quarterly publication of the Linguistic Society of America. Contains scholarly articles on various aspects of linguistic science; book reviews, bibliographies, charts, etc. Cumulative index every five years. Supplemented by two series of occasional publications: *Language Monographs* and *Language Dissertations.* Indexed in *Linguistic Bibliography, Annual bibliography of English Language and Literature,* also in *Psychological Abstracts.*

Language and Speech. London. v. 1, 1958- . **322**

Quarterly. Contains scholarly articles devoted to fundamental problems in language and speech in all their psychological, physiological and physical aspects. Includes book reviews, charts, bibliographies and indexes. Indexed in *MLA International Bibliography*, and in *Psychological Abstracts*.

323   *Language Learning.* Ann Arbor, Mich. v. 1, 1948- .

"A Quarterly Journal of Applied Linguistics", published by University of Michigan. Devoted to the improvement of foreign language learning and teaching. Deals with general descriptive linguistics, descriptions of specific languages, descriptive comparisons of two or more languages, the language of children, bilingualism, the teaching of general linguistics, the teaching of specific languages, teaching methods and educational experiments. Carries book reviews, notes and bibliographies. Indexed in *Language and Language Behavior Abstracts* and in *Education Index*.

324   *Language Research in Progress.* Washington, D. C. 1965- .

Semi-annual publication of the Center for Applied Linguistics. Aims to assist scholars by collecting and disseminating information about all aspects of current language research, in the U. S. and abroad. Every report supersedes the previous one. Divided in three parts, it gives main and sub-categories, names of research personnel and institutions by state or country, names and addresses of individual contributors and titles of their projects.

325   *Language Sciences.* Bloomington, Ind. 1968- .

An occasional, interdisciplinary publication meant to inform about new developments in psycholinguistics, sociolinguistics, applied linguistics, formal languages, stylistics and animal communication; new projects, meetings, etc., both in the U. S. and abroad; issued by the Research Center for the Language Sciences of Indiana University. Stresses reviews of new literature. Includes bibliographies on various topics. Indexed in *MLA International Bibliography*.

326   *Lingua.* Amsterdam. v. 1, 1948- .

"International Review of General Linguistics", published quarterly. Aims to be of interest to any linguist, whatever his own specialization. Includes book reviews, notes on conferences, linguistic maps, charts, bibliographies and indexes.

Indexed in *Linguistic Bibliography* and in *Language and Language Behavior Abstracts.*

Linguistic Inquiry. Boston, Mass. v. 1, 1970- .　　　**327**

Quarterly. Scholarly publication of the Massachusetts Institute of Technology, with Noam Chomsky and Roam Jakobson on the Advisory Editorial Board. Attempts to present new theories as they develop, and to provide an intellectual platform for the exchange of ideas in the field of linguistics and related fields of anthropology, acoustics, biology, literature, mathematics, philosophy, psychology, and the psychopathology of language. Includes an interesting section: "Squibs and Discussion".

Linguistic Reporter. Washington, D. C. v. 1, 1959- .　　**328**

Bi-monthly, issued by the Center for Applied Linguistics. Deals with the application of linguistic science, in all its aspects, to practical language problems. Contains few long feature articles and numerous short notices on recent book and periodical publications. Reports on national and international congresses, meetings, seminars, special projects, scholarly exchange programs and on papers in progress. Includes a column "Linguists wanted". Carries bibliographies, indexes, illustrations. Excellent publication, useful to both linguists and general readers. Indexed in *MLA International Bibliography, Annual Bibliography of English Language and Literature,* and in *Language and Language Behavior Abstracts.*

LINGUISTIC SOCIETY OF AMERICA. *Meeting Handbook.*　**329**
Washington, D. C. 1965- .

Prepared by the Center for Applied Linguistics as guides for persons attending annual conferences, and meant as permanent records of papers presented at meetings, these handbooks contain official programs, abstracts of papers, and author, or title listings.

Linguistics. The Hague. v. 1, 1963- .　　　　　**330**

"An International Review", appears approximately nine times a year. Contains scholarly articles and book reviews dealing with all aspects of language and linguistics. Includes notices on international conferences; charts, tables, etc. Text in English, French and German. Indexed in *Linguistic Bibliography,* also in *Language and Language Behavior Abstracts.*

331 *Mechanical Translation.* Chicago. v. 1, 1958- .

Quarterly, published by the Association for Machine Translation and Computational Linguistics. Highly specialized, it deals with technical problems of automatic translation and stresses its mathematical and logical aspects. Indexed in *Linguistic Bibliography,* also in *Science Citation Index.*

332 MODERN LANGUAGE ASSOCIATION OF AMERICA. *Publications.* Menasha, Wisc. v. 1, 1884- .

Published seven times a year. Includes scholarly, literary and linguistic, papers by the members of the Association; proceedings of meetings and conferences; surveys; directories of members; rules and regulations. Until 1970 the June issue contained the *Annual bibliography.* (Now the contents of the bibliography are divided into four volumes and published jointly by the Modern Language Association of America and the Pennsylvania State University.) A cumulative index for 1884-1935 was published in 1936, and for 1936-1964 in 1966.

333 *Modern Language Journal.* Ann Arbor, Mich. v. 1, 1916- .

Issued eight times a year by the National Federation of Modern Language Teachers Associations, it is an excellent publication "devoted primarily to methods, pedagogical research, and to topics of professional interest to all language teachers." Includes book reviews, notes on national and international conferences, announcements of new publications, bibliographies, charts, tables; annual indexes. Indexed in *Annual Bibliography of English Language and Literature, Linguistic Bibliography,* also in *Education Index.*

334 *Modern Languages.* London. v. 1, 1905- .

Quarterly publication of the Modern Language Association. Contains articles and book reviews on contemporary European literature and on techniques in language teaching and learning. Includes bibliographies, notes on conferences and advertisements. Text mainly in English. Indexed in *MLA International Bibliography, The Year's Work in Modern Language Studies,* also in *British Education Index.*

P. M. L. A. *See* MODERN LANGUAGE ASSOCIATION OF AMERICA. *Publications.*

PHILOLOGICAL SOCIETY. London. *Transactions.* 1854- .   **335**

Important series of scholarly publications on linguistic research, worldwide coverage. Especially significant since the introduction of J. R. Firth's theory of the phonological structure in his paper *Sounds and Prosodies,* in 1948. Included are bibliographies, reports, proceedings and lists of members of the Philological Society.

Phonetica. Basel. v. 1, 1957- .   **336**

"International Journal of Phonetics", published quarterly (2 vols. of 4 issues per year). Contains scholarly articles and book reviews dealing with all aspects of speech and speech disorders. Includes bibliographies and indexes. Indexed in *Linguistic Bibliography* and in *Language and Language Behavior Abstracts.*

Quarterly Checklist of Linguistics. Darien, Conn. v. 1, 1958- .   **337**

International index of current books, monographs, brochures and separates published by American Bibliographic Service. Includes translations, reprints, revised editions and paperbacks in Western languages. Lists prices and publishers' addresses. Contains indexes of authors, editors and translators.

Quarterly Journal of Speech. New York. v. 1, 1915- .   **338**

Scholarly publication of Speech Association of America. Deals with rhetorical theory and criticism, group communication and public speaking, theatre arts and drama criticism, speech pathology, behavioral sciences, etc. Includes book reviews, announcements of new publications, indexes. Indexed in *Linguistic Bibliography, MLA International Bibliography, Annual Bibliography of English Language and Literature* and in *Education Index*.

339   *Studia Linguistica*. Lund, Sweden. v. 1, 1947- .

Semi-annual journal dealing with problems of general and comparative linguistics. Contains scholarly articles, book reviews, bibliographies, charts, diagrams, etc. Text in French, English and German. Indexed in *Linguistic Bibliography, MLA International Bibliography*, and in *Language and Language Behavior Abstracts*.

340   *Studies in Linguistics*. Dallas, Texas. v. 1, 1942- .

Quarterly, published by the Anthropology Research Center at Southern Methodist University. Devoted to research in anthropological linguistics, this journal contains scholarly articles, bibliographies and book reviews, cumulative indexes every five years. Supplemented by *Occasional papers*. Indexed in *Social Sciences & Humanities Index, MLA International Bibliography*, also in *Language and Language Behavior Abstracts*.

341   *Travaux du Cercle Linguistique de Prague*. Prague. v. 1, 1929-v. 8, 1939.

Important series containing works of members of the Circle (Praźský linguistický krouźek), many of which were presented at international congresses of linguists. Ceased publication with volume 8, 1939, put out in honour of Prince Trubetzkoy. Superseded by *Travaux Linguistiques de Prague* in 1964. See below.

342   *Travaux Linguistiques de Prague*. Prague. v. 1, 1964- .

Internationally recognized publication of the Czechoslovak Academy of Sciences devoted to theory of language and research in linguistics, particularly to phonology. Each of the three volumes issued since 1954 contains over twenty papers. Individual titles in the series go as follows: v. 1. L'Ecole de Prague d'aujourd'hui; v. 2. Les problèmes du centre et de la périphérie du système de la langue; v. 3. Etudes structurales dédiées au VIe Congrès des slavistes. Articles, written in English, French, German and Russian, contain charts and diagrams. The series are simultaneously reprinted in the United States by the University of Alabama Press.

Travaux du Cercle Linguistique de Copenhague. Copenhagen, E. **343** Munksgaard. no. 1, 1944- .

Irregular series issued under the auspices of the Linguistic Circle of Copenhagen. Important, international in scope, these papers and monographs cover all aspects of language and linguistics from ancient times to the present day. Bibliographies included. Text in French, English and German.

Word. New York. v. 1, 1945- . **344**

"Journal of the Linguistic Circle of New York", published three times per annum; during recent years very irregular. General in aim, it deals with all aspects of linguistics. Includes bibliographies, book reviews, indexes, and occasional Monographs as supplements to various volumes of *Word.* Text in English and French. Indexed in *The Year's Work in Modern Language Studies,* also in *Language and Language Behavior Abstracts.*

AUTHOR INDEX

Includes editors and a few selected dictionary titles
(References are to entry numbers.)

PERIODICALS AND SERIES INDEX

Includes serial bibliographies, abstracts, indexes and theses
(References are to entry numbers.)